HEALTHCARE LEADERSHIP
AND RURAL
COMMUNITIES

Challenges, Strategies, and Solutions

HEALTHCARE LEADERSHIP AND RURAL COMMUNITIES

Challenges, Strategies, and Solutions

Tim Putnam, Nikki King,
and Bill Auxier

ACHE Management Series

Library of Congress Cataloging-in-Publication Data
Names: Putnam, Tim (Timothy), author. | King, Nikki, author. | Auxier, William R., author.
Title: Healthcare leadership and rural communities : challenges, strategies, and solutions / Tim Putnam, Nikki King, and Bill Auxier. Other titles: Management series (Ann Arbor, Mich.)
Description: Chicago : Health Administration Press, 2023. | Series: ACHE management series | Includes bibliographical references. | Summary: "Leaders of rural healthcare organizations confront unique challenges. Payment systems, power dynamics, labor availability, and accessible resources differ considerably between rural and urban areas. Healthcare Leadership and Rural Communities outlines what it takes to manage care in a rural community and provides advice on overcoming the common challenges that healthcare executives confront. The authors provide candid insights gained from their experience as rural healthcare managers and their work with leaders in the field" – Provided by publisher.
Identifiers: LCCN 2023001884 | ISBN 9781640553750 (trade paperback) | ISBN 9781640553743 (epub) | ISBN 9781640553989 (ebook)
Subjects: MESH: Rural Health Services—organization & administration | Leadership | BISAC: MEDICAL / Hospital Administration & Care | BUSINESS & ECONOMICS / Industries / Healthcare
Classification: LCC RA771.5 | NLM WA 390 | DDC 362.1/04257—dc23/eng/20230526
LC record available at https://lccn.loc.gov/2023001884

The paper used in this publication meets the minimum requirements of American National Standard for Information Sciences—Permanence of Paper for Printed Library Materials, ANSI Z39.48-1984. ∞ ™

Acquisitions editor: La'Toya Carter; Manuscript editor: Joe Pixler; Cover designer: Mark Oberkrom; Layout: Integra

Found an error or a typo? We want to know! Please e-mail it to hapbooks@ache.org, mentioning the book's title and putting "Book Error" in the subject line.

For photocopying and copyright information, please contact Copyright Clearance Center at www.copyright.com or at (978) 750-8400.

Health Administration Press
A division of the Foundation of the American
    College of Healthcare Executives
300 S. Riverside Plaza, Suite 1900
Chicago, IL 60606-6698
(312) 424-2800

This book is dedicated to the people in rural healthcare who selflessly serve their neighbors in small towns across America. They wish for no personal honor or recognition, but instead want only to make the world better for those they serve. Healthcare leaders should consider themselves lucky if they get a chance to work with people who are driven to make life better for people in rural America.

In writing this book, my favorite conversations were with clinicians, community members, staff, and other leaders who were frustrated with the status quo and knew healthcare could be better. They freely shared their ideas and concepts to help move the care we provide forward.

Rural healthcare is filled with heroes and villains, the humble and the proud . . . people seeking money and glory as well as those dedicated to serving their fellow man. Most truly want to make a positive impact on their communities, and I consider myself blessed to work with them. They make rural America a very special place.

Tim Putnam, DHA, MBA, FACHE

Contents

Preface

RURAL HEALTH LEADERSHIP is not for the faint of heart! Leading rural healthcare organizations is challenging at the best of times. Rural leaders deal with limited resources, difficulty in recruiting clinical staff, and a distant voice in state and federal policy decisions. And everyone in a small town—patients, providers, and community leaders—seems to know everyone else's business. Compounding these factors is the pressure from knowing that failure means lives and livelihoods are at stake and that closure of a rural health facility can signal the slow and steady decline of an entire community.

This book addresses the challenges faced by rural leaders from a practical perspective. It offers guidance on how to work through the predicaments that leaders find themselves in and shares practical solutions.

Healthcare teams, boards, providers, and community leaders can use this book as a resource to learn together. The information is presented in a way that can prompt shared reflection on how to apply it to their specific circumstances. Seeing parallels between scenarios and case studies described in the book and local challenges can be a good way to open a conversation about a difficult topic and then work toward a solution.

Rural healthcare desperately needs good leaders. People who are committed to making a positive impact on the lives of their neighbors will find the calling of rural health leadership personally and professionally impactful and rewarding. Hopefully, this book will give them the guidance and support they will need.

Introduction

MANY PEOPLE WORKING in rural healthcare struggle with the difficulties associated with serving the needs of small communities. There is a simple reason the task seems so hard: It *is* very hard. Payment models designed for high-volume urban centers, regulations and standards written by people who work in huge academic settings, and limited resources are just a few of the myriad reasons that rural medical institutions struggle to survive.

Even as rural hospitals are shuttered at a quickening pace, many that remain open must discontinue vital services that have a negative return on investment like obstetrics to stay in business. Meanwhile, rural independent physicians who are unable to make money with their practices have closed their offices and joined the local clinic or hospital. This consolidation of services figuratively puts all the community's healthcare eggs into one basket, so if its lone organization closes, the staff has no viable option but to leave town for employment—and the community loses all local access to care.

Rural healthcare leaders are under tremendous pressure to maintain high-quality care *and* financial viability. They may be seen as money-grubbing administrators who deprive valiant clinicians of the resources they need to heal their patients, and yet the failure of the business will signal the inevitable decline of its community.

Without a doubt, the job of a rural healthcare leader is not for the faint of heart. The people who choose to take on the role and take it seriously are warriors. They are committed to making a positive impact on the community they serve. To help them demonstrate their commitment, this book outlines practical strategies and tactics. Six themes predominate.

1.   **Technology brings opportunities and challenges.**
     Changes in healthcare delivery have significant
     implications (some positive, some negative) for rural
     healthcare. Telehealth and telemedicine can bring
     advanced care to remote areas where subspecialties,
     imaging technology, proton beams, and robotic surgery
     would not otherwise be available. Because scale and
     expense requirements effectively eliminate the ability of
     rural organizations to possess every tool and capability they
     need, rural healthcare leaders must collaborate with the
     organizations that have them.

2.   **Everyone works better together.** Communities can
     thrive when everyone works together. Rural healthcare
     leaders must be teambuilders. When emergency medical
     services (EMS) providers, hospitals, clinics, long-term care
     providers, and employers all work exclusively in their self-
     interests, the consequences will likely be negative for all.
     If an employer opts to save money by going with a health
     plan's preferred network of out-of-town providers, local
     clinics and practices may be forced to scale back services or
     close.

3.   **Resources are limited, by design.** The way healthcare
     costs are reimbursed in the United States effectively
     disenfranchises rural care delivery. The costs to prepare
     for whatever crisis might occur are not reimbursed; they
     are only paid for care provided—and there are generally
     too few patients to cover the costs.

4.   **Readiness is essential regardless of low volume.**
     Despite the reality of inconsistent and somewhat
     unpredictable volume that rural healthcare organizations
     face, every program or service requires some level of
     capital investment and ongoing operational cost support.
     Maintaining rural EMS with ambulance, equipment, and
     staff is expensive, and every day that goes by without a

single call is a day without revenue to support the service. However, not providing quality service comes at a greater human cost to the community.

5.   **It's good to know who's who.** In a small town, familial and social connections are abundant and not always obvious. Making a hiring decision based solely on merit can have negative repercussions if people with deep roots in the community perceive any disrespect. Successful leaders must be aware of these connections so they can anticipate the impact of their decisions on themselves and their organization.

6.   **The joys of experiencing and improving rural life.** Despite all the challenges of rural healthcare, its leaders enjoy the unique ability to make a huge impact on their friends and neighbors—to improve the quality of life for people they know and care about.

There is a lot of "rural" across the United States. While many similarities exist, no two rural communities are exactly alike. Small towns pride themselves on individuality, and rural healthcare organizations tend to follow that attitude.

While reading this book, it's important to keep in mind that each local situation is unique. It's advisable to share the ideas in this book with other stakeholders to see what rings true or how situations may differ. Clinicians may disagree with a particular perspective, while administrators wholeheartedly concur. The reflection points at the end of each chapter are intended to prompt lively discussions of common challenges and lead to collaborative solutions.

CHAPTER 1

The Unique Realities of Rural Healthcare Leadership

Bill Auxier, PhD, and Tim Putnam, DHA, MBA, FACHE

BOB, THE HOSPITAL CEO, was filling up his pickup truck at the local gas station when the mother of one of the girls on his daughter's softball team approached him in a shy, awkward way. After saying hello, she asked, "Could you write a prescription for me?" She knew he was the president of the hospital and assumed he was a physician. Bob replied that although he did work at the hospital, he was not a physician and could not write prescriptions. "Who is your doctor?" he asked helpfully. "Let's give them a call."

This scene illustrates a common experience for rural healthcare leaders: As the public face of healthcare in the community, they are recognized everywhere. Their unique status is also what makes them leaders in the community, even as they face extraordinary demands of providing healthcare services with limited resources. And yet, with these challenges of leadership come opportunities.

THE RURAL LEADERSHIP REALITY

Context is worth noting here: Every 3–4 weeks, another rural community loses its hospital, and as the number of hospitals in rural America continues to drop, the people who depend on them are getting older, poorer, and sicker on average than their urban counterparts (Foundation for Research on Equal Opportunity 2021). New rural healthcare leaders inherit that reality upon arrival in town, along with the opportunity to make an impact on these issues. They are in a special position to make sure that their communities continue to have access to the care they deserve.

How does a rural healthcare leader make a positive impact? First, by redefining healthcare. Instead of focusing solely on illness and injury, they work toward ensuring the health and well-being of the population. They address acute care but also work with community leaders to improve the local social determinants of health such as safe housing, transportation, healthy foods, and so forth to deliver value for all patients. They tie the work to improve the health of the entire community—population health—to their organization's mission statement. Proactive leaders incorporate population health into their strategic plans and then secure the resources that are necessary to fulfill them. This requires collaboration with other organizations, groups, and leaders.

No Anonymity

Like Bob at the gas station, rural healthcare leaders have no anonymity. Everyone in a small town pretty much knows everyone else—and if they do not know who you are, they will find out. Strangers are obvious. The CEO of Cleveland Clinic can walk down the street and most people will not pay much attention. But if the CEO of Hamilton Memorial Hospital in southern Illinois walks down the street, everyone will take note and wonder where they are headed.

In the absence of anonymity, people see no problem with approaching rural healthcare leaders at the high school basketball game or in the local grocery store and putting them on the spot: *My neighbor was at the hospital yesterday. How are they doing?* Or, *I heard that Dr. Henderson is pretty frustrated. Is she leaving town?* Of course, privacy regulations put most of these conversations out of bounds, but they still happen. Simply hiding behind regulations may help in many cases, but some people will push hard to find out what they want to know. It's good to be prepared to direct them to sources such as family members who can address their questions.

The constant burden of public access may seem unfair, but it is part of a healthcare leader's big role in a small community, and family members must share the burden. Several basic rules and realities apply.

- **Everyone is fair game.** Employees won't hesitate to address work issues, wherever they may be. Leaders may be pulled into serious and confidential conversations even when they are out with their families.
- **Keep it confidential.** When someone asks family members about what is really going on at the hospital, even the most innocuous inside information can lead to problems. Saying that the CEO or CFO is working late because an audit is taking longer than expected could raise unfounded concerns about financial viability or impropriety when people do not understand that audits are routine.
- **People get angry.** Emotions can run hot in healthcare, and healthcare leaders may take the brunt of people's anger following the unexpected death of their loved one at the hospital or the termination of a hospital employee. Such public scenes are rare, but it is important to anticipate them and be prepared to quickly and quietly move family members away from any confrontation.

This familiarity isn't all bad. It also presents rural healthcare leaders with the great opportunity to take special care of their neighbors. Rather than a patient with a number, a person in a rural hospital is a fellow church member, relative, friend, or friend of a friend. So, not only do rural healthcare leaders see the impact they are making on the health of their community, they also personally know the individuals they are serving. This distinctive status presents an opportunity to clearly see the difference they make with their work every day.

Community Leadership

As the scene with Bob at the gas station demonstrates, rural healthcare leaders are, by default, also go-to leaders of their community. And as community leaders, they are obligated to set an example. When initial COVID-19 vaccinations were first recommended by public health officials, members of the community noticed when their local hospital CEO was not publicly rolling up their own sleeves. Walking the talk is crucial in creating and supporting a healthy culture.

Resource Stewardship

From an operational perspective, there is at least one special reward for leading a hospital in a rural community: Action to meet local needs can be taken without going through a lot of red tape. With fewer corporate stakeholders, leaders can gain consensus on a new concept or program in a relatively short period of time. While large urban hospitals are like cruise ships, their small rural counterparts can function like ski boats. Their ability to change course is much more manageable.

Tempering that freedom is the fact that rural hospitals, especially the independents, have very limited resources. The breadth of experience and expertise in clinical specialties as well as nonclinical areas (e.g., finance, marketing, computer systems, contracting, purchasing) is typically thin. A rural healthcare leader may not be able to build up sufficient staffing to delegate certain projects or tasks like an urban healthcare leader can. More must be done with less. While frustrating, this challenge also presents a tremendous opportunity to expand one's knowledge base and skill set. The leader may need to decide whether to fund an obstetrics program or an addiction treatment program, even though the community needs both. People's lives are at stake.

Challenges present opportunities for collaboration through innovative thinking. Bringing together diverse viewpoints of care providers at the hospital as well as local government entities, schools, community groups, and faith-based organizations—even competing providers—for brainstorming sessions can identify creative ways to support local population health efforts. The more that leaders collaborate, the more they can innovate.

Resources for Rural CEOs and Other Leaders

Given the challenges and lack of local resources, rural healthcare leaders must work with others in their field to find solutions to common problems.

National Rural Health Association (NRHA) certification programs created specifically for rural CEOs as well as CFOs and CNOs (www.crhleadership.com) can help them effectively deal with the special challenges in rural healthcare. Networking is helpful, too. National organizations such as the NRHA facilitate collaboration among leaders who are knowledgeable, honest, and open to sharing both successes and failures. With so many small communities struggling across the nation, there is a good chance that someone has found a solution to any given challenge.

- Federal Office of Rural Health Rural Health Research Centers, www.ruralhealthresearch.org
- National Association of Rural Health Clinics, www.narch.org
- National Rural Health Association, www.ruralhealth.us
- National Rural Health Resource Center, www.ruralcenter.org
- Rural Health Information Hub, www.ruralhealthinfo.org

The COVID-19 pandemic exacerbated many of the resource challenges that rural healthcare leaders had already been dealing with every day, such as recruiting and retaining the professional staff required to safely serve a rural community. Rural healthcare physicians have been leaving the field at an unprecedented rate for a variety of reasons, notably burnout, while nurses have been drawn to higher-paying traveling positions.

More physicians and nurses are sorely needed. Collaboration can provide a solution to this challenge. For example, six rural hospitals coordinated their approach to recruiting family medicine doctors. By pooling resources, the hospitals were able to fly in the prospects who were finishing their residencies so they could personally experience everything the organizations and communities had to offer. The efforts helped to recruit 20 physicians (Mead 2021).

THE VALUE OF VISIBILITY

To build valuable goodwill, rural healthcare leaders should live in the community and be part of its life. When an absentee CEO lives somewhere else, everyone will know they are not "one of us." To be vested members of the community, leaders must be present and mourn when the community loses someone, cheer for victories, and fight to make life better. They must be seen buying a car locally and keeping the dealer's sticker on the bumper, shopping at the farmers' market, frequenting fish fries and chili cookoffs, and attending ball games—wearing the local school colors with pride on game days. If they expect people to stay local for their healthcare, rural healthcare leaders must reinforce that concept with their own actions.

Internal visibility is important, too. Staff members in rural areas are frequently asked what their boss is like. A leader who has established personal or casual interactions with their staff enables them to answer those questions. Rural hospitals can have as few as 100 employees, rarely more than 2,000; rural clinics and long-term care facilities typically have even fewer—the "we are all on the same team" ideal is definitely achievable in small towns.

Of course, with relatively few people working at a rural facility, the chance of staff being overwhelmed is significant. Leaders who are unaware or appear uncaring when their staff is swamped risk losing team morale. Building a strong team takes continuous hard work, which can be lost with one thoughtless or selfish action.

Staff Connection Tactics

There are many practical tactics to help rural healthcare leaders connect with staff.

- **Don't park in an executive spot.** The logic behind executive parking is sound: Frequent offsite meetings can demand multiple trips to the parking lot. However, the walk to and from general staff parking areas is rarely long, and taking those extra steps visibly reinforces the same-team ideal. The walk can also lead to useful informal interactions with staff that would not happen otherwise.
- **Find a way to be useful.** Knowing how to help and being able to step in when a department is slammed can make a big impression. For executives from clinical backgrounds, keeping licenses and certifications current and maintaining skills may be difficult, but the efforts are worthwhile. Leaders who do not come from a clinical background can find ways to help, too. For example, they can learn how to transport patients when the clinical staff is caring for other patients.
- **Spring for pizza.** When staff is overwhelmed and there is no way to assist with their work, providing food may be the best gesture. It can mean a lot to people who are working long hours without a break.

- **Do rounding.** Walking through all departments to interact with the staff (following departmental guidelines) or just being attentive to their work is a great way to see how things are going. It's important to get away from the desk to learn exactly why the staff is working so hard. They may say *Everything is great,* which is code for *We don't want the boss to know what we are doing and mess up our day.* Or, they may say *Everything is bad,* which is code for *The only way to get what we want is to be a squeaky wheel.* Ideally, though, staff will feel comfortable telling the boss that things are good when they are good and bad when they are bad. This requires the development of a trusting relationship over time.

- **Serve lunch.** In addition to eating at the cafeteria, occasionally taking an hour or two to serve lunch can make for an enjoyable break from the routine. Serving can also provide dozens of informal interactions with staff. It takes a few times for people to recognize that this is not a gimmick and take advantage of this opportunity to interact with administration.

CEO TURNOVER

CEO turnover is a special challenge in rural healthcare. The authors know of one hospital that went through nine CEOs in 10 years, and there are many similar stories. Competitors may take advantage of disruption at the top of an organization by recruiting its staff and physicians, which may increase the likelihood of other senior executives leaving, too. As a result, many important strategic activities must be delayed, if not canceled, which can leave a hospital and its community struggling.

The short tenures of rural CEOs have many causes but generally come down to the challenges noted in this chapter. They have to make a lot of hard decisions, and in a small town, people feel the effects of those decisions directly and take them personally. Either by choice or force, embattled CEOs decide that leaving is best for them and their family.

LEADER BURNOUT

Burnout has always been an issue in healthcare, but the COVID-19 pandemic and subsequent financial pressures have added several exclamation points to the scourge. Helping staff deal with the stress that leads to burnout is essential, especially in light of personnel shortages that will continue for years.

Before they can take care of others, rural healthcare leaders need to take care of themselves and develop a strategic plan to prevent their own burnout. Simply booking a weeklong vacation a couple of times a year will not suffice. The steps necessary to relieve the pressure will vary among individuals, but in any case, the steps must be purposeful.

It's always important to maintain a strong body, mind, and spirit—engaging in regular exercise, eating a healthy diet, and welcoming the support of close friends are always good starters for that approach. With their personal physicians' approval, leaders who are swimming in the fishbowl of rural healthcare may find relief in a variety of ways.

- Strenuous exercise or activity that requires intense concentration can allow the mind to escape for a while from the day's hard decisions.
- While it is important to frequent local establishments, an occasional dinner or weekend out of town is a nice way to spend time, anonymously.
- National and state health conferences provide good opportunities to get out of town and meet with others facing similar challenges. They are also good venues for seeing local challenges from a different perspective.

Purposeful getaways are vital for well-being, but they require some preparation to ensure that they don't add stress.

- Empowering one or two individuals to make decisions will limit the interruptions to a break and provide an opportunity to assess their management skills.
- With a safety-valve contact process in place, the person or people empowered to be in charge temporarily can be designated as the only points of contact with specific instructions of when to call. For example, if Dr. X shows up to his shift impaired and assaults the nursing supervisor, a call is probably warranted. This system won't stop physicians, board members, or community leaders from reaching out during a break but will decrease less important calls and e-mails about more routine matters.

REFLECTION POINTS

- How are you and your family prepared to deal with awkward or potentially problematic questions from the public?
- What one thing could you do to be a more effective community leader?
- How can you tell when work pressures are affecting your staff's life or work?
- How can you tell when work pressures are affecting your life or work?
- Is there someone to whom you can honestly admit that the pressure is getting to be too much?
- What steps might help when the pressures of leadership get to be too much?

REFERENCES

Foundation for Research on Equal Opportunity (blog); "The Most Vulnerable Patients Are Rural Americans," by Mark Dornauer, posted March 27, 2020, updated November 16, 2021. https://freopp.org/the-most-vulnerable-patients-are-rural-americans-c5bb4f8e9217.

Mead, A. 2021. "It Takes a Village: Rural Recruitment and Retention." *The Rural Monitor.* Published November 3. https://www.rural-healthinfo.org/rural-monitor/rural-recruitment-and-retention/.

CHAPTER 2

Quality Matters

Tim Putnam, DHA, MBA, FACHE, and Nikki King, DHA

CONTINUALLY IMPROVING THE quality of care and the outcomes that patients receive should be high on every healthcare leader's list of priorities. High quality builds trust within the community and pride in the organization. A rural healthcare leader's role and responsibilities with quality assurance can be assessed by the following:

- **Monitoring.** Effective monitoring processes need to be in place. If quality metrics cannot be measured, it is virtually impossible to determine if quality is improving or getting worse.

- **Team engagement.** Quality cannot come from one person or department. Everyone needs to be engaged in delivering better care. The best situation is when all eyes are on the process and everyone is actively committed to making things better.

- **Quality standardization.** The focal point should not be the best outcome that can be achieved, It should be the improvement in overall quality and consistency of care. Excellent care on the day shift during the week is great, but if there is not the same quality on a weekend night, does it matter? Patients cannot control when they will suffer trauma or go into labor. They deserve the same quality care regardless of the time or day they arrive.

- **Provider variation.** A worthy quality goal is to have the worst provider in the organization achieve the same outcome as the best provider.
- **Equity.** As the primary local access point for healthcare, rural organizations are generally responsible for the health of their entire community. Rural leaders must include equity in the quality discussion. The vision of quality cannot be limited to great care for those who can afford it or those we deem worthy.

Staff and providers must be able to see quality of care as their priority and continually work to improve it. Therefore, leadership must focus more on where quality is headed rather than where it is today.

Many quality measures are written with high-volume centers in mind; they rarely reflect the quality of rural facilities with any accuracy. For example, serious surgery complications may be relatively rare, but for a rural hospital with few surgical procedures, a year may pass with no significant complications. Through that lens, the hospital looks perfect. Conversely, with a low surgical volume, just one complication makes the hospital look horrid.

Basic Quality Measures

Several standard quality measures related to certain functions, processes, and complications can be applied at high enough volumes in rural facilities to be meaningful. Examples of these measurements are:

- aspirin for chest pain for patients upon arrival to the emergency and inpatient departments;
- emergency department (ED) transfer communications;

- combined inpatient and outpatient prophylactic antibiotic timing for surgery;
- patient urinary tract infection and catheter use; and
- use of tPA for ischemic stroke patients.

Source: Casey et al. 2012

Other indicators that are used to determine quality are more difficult to standardize for a rural health system, which makes monitoring for trends more important. For instance, a typical standard for average door-to-balloon (DtB) time for ST-elevation myocardial infarction patients is 90 minutes. This is the time from the patient's arrival with a heart attack requiring cardiac angioplasty intervention to the time when the angioplasty balloon is inflated. This standard makes sense when the catheter lab and ED are in the same building and there is a team on call 24/7. But what should the standard DtB time be when the lab is 50 or 100 miles away? This variability creates a significant challenge when it comes to judging quality at a rural hospital against that of tertiary systems or even other rural hospitals. The variables of obtaining transportation and coordination with the catheter lab complicate the calculation for quality. Every ED needs to monitor its own DtB time and work to improve it, but comparing rural hospitals to other types of hospitals is simply not viable using this metric.

Leaders need to understand their role in these situations. Here, leaders can

- establish a smooth process with the receiving hospital for accepting patients,
- support the care team by ensuring seamless transfers of patients and their records,
- encourage the receiving facility to regularly share data on patient outcomes and ways to improve the process.

URBAN VS. RURAL QUALITY

It is too commonly assumed that rural hospitals provide lower quality care in comparison to urban hospitals. Rural facilities do have far fewer resources and case volumes than their larger urban counterparts, and rural patients with the most complex needs are typically transferred to those urban hospitals. But the truth of the assumption really depends on what quality means and how it is measured.

Take, for example, primary care physicians in a rural area who do not have endocrinologists, psychiatrists, pulmonologists, or other specialists readily available to call on as needed. Because of transportation challenges for many rural patients, referral to specialists is generally difficult and frequently impossible. Should the average hemoglobin A1C level for the patients of a primary care physician be compared to that of the diabetic patients of an urban endocrinologist? If a rural primary care physician refuses to see complex diabetic patients and instead makes a referral that a patient is unable to fulfill, the quality scores for the physician would be better—but how would the patient fare? It is difficult to truly assess quality and virtually impossible for the patient to make this assessment.

Every organization should effectively monitor quality and work to improve it, without gaming the system or getting caught in a battle of "who's best." It is vital to center efforts on improving the actual quality of every episode of care, not just the quality scores.

INSIDE QUALITY VS. OUTCOMES QUALITY

Rural facilities seldom have all the resources necessary to provide complex treatments today. Back when treatment protocols were less advanced, it was possible to work only on improving the care inside the facility itself. Patients were not transferred for care as frequently because care could typically be provided independently. Today, care teams may be drawn from public health, emergency medical services, and tertiary facilities to achieve quality patient outcomes.

The work toward better overall patient outcomes requires leadership collaboration with other organizations. The DtB example illustrates the need for this type of effort. The quality of the outcomes the patients receive is only partly the result of the caliber of care delivered at the rural facility. If there is no ability to transfer the patient (e.g., fog prohibits air ambulances from flying, or the only transfer ambulance is carrying another patient), several hours may pass before a patient can get to the catheter lab. How should that be reflected in the hospital's quality of care? Whose responsibility is it to ensure that patients can get to where they need to be? Rural health leaders must take ownership of this role and consider the patient's outcome, not just the part that occurs inside their facilities. They are the only ones who can create solid relationships and collaborative efforts to make complex care integration possible.

WORKING RELATIONSHIPS WITH TERTIARY HOSPITALS

Every provider is proud of the work they do to make a difference in patients' lives. That confidence in competence is essential. How can a surgeon cut into a patient to remove an infected appendix without the confidence that the patient will receive excellent care?

A common refrain among healthcare leaders is that there are 5,000 hospitals in the United States and each one is a "Top 100" hospital, according to their billboards. Every leader wants to be proud of their team's work. However, this self-confidence can create a degree of arrogance. Pride in one's work tends to come out as disdain for the work of others. Transferred patients frequently infer that they have received inferior care at the rural hospital when they hear comments like *Thank goodness you were brought here! Had you stayed at your local hospital, you would have died.* The patient and family may understand this to mean that they were lucky to survive the substandard care at the rural hospital. The comment actually means that the rural hospital did a great job at diagnosing the condition and getting the patient the advanced care they needed.

Working with urban, tertiary hospitals is fraught with complexity. (Chapter 6 goes deep into that topic.) However, established solid working relationships are vital for patient care even when the tertiary facility is aggressively competing with the rural hospital for patients, staff, and other resources.

It's widely believed that the best chance to survive trauma is to get to a Level 1 trauma center as quickly as possible. This belief leaves many to assume that only the highest level of care is ever appropriate, and anything below that level is inferior. It is true that rural hospitals typically do not have the sophisticated equipment or clinical subspecialists that tertiary facilities possess. And yet, rural hospitals can play a vital role in caring for patients who cannot survive the long trip to a higher level of care without the interventions provided at the local hospital.

There are also some points to consider when the care team is deciding whether to transfer a patient and where to send them.

- **Patient choice.** If the patient has a preferred tertiary hospital, their wishes must be followed. This is particularly difficult when their choice is a hospital where the transfer process is cumbersome or its location is far away and the travel will significantly delay vital care.

- **Predatory practices by tertiary hospitals.** It is not uncommon for a tertiary receiving hospital to use navigator services for patients arriving in their ED. For example, a patient arriving with an acute condition from a newly diagnosed cancer is steered to the hospital's oncology program and follow-up care even when the rural hospital has a solid oncology program.

- **Negative comments about the rural facility.** When patients are told that their lab tests that were just performed at the rural hospital must be repeated at

the tertiary hospital, they could assume there was
something wrong with the rural hospital's capability.
They may not know that repeating tests to determine
the progression of the disease is commonplace,
that there is a problem with the transfer of records,
or that the tertiary hospital is following a specific
protocol that requires a different test.

Rural healthcare leaders must realize that streamlined processes
and clear communication channels with referral centers must be in
place before they are needed for patient care. All too often, rural
clinicians must create a referral process for their patients in the midst
of a health crisis for their patient. They must find transportation
and a receiving facility or a physician that will accept the patient,
then transmit test results, their diagnosis, treatments, and myriad
other details. Leaders who work to make this process easier for providers will see a positive impact on patient outcomes and provider
satisfaction.

The determination of which patients should stay and which
should be transferred requires awareness of a facility's capabilities.
The best rural facilities routinely review and evaluate the cases
of patients who were transferred to confirm whether the transfers were appropriate. Creating a team of clinicians to carefully
review trends in transfers can help identify additional equipment,
training, or service lines that could possibly keep more patients
local for care. Complex cases of patients who are kept should be
reviewed to determine if superior care could have been provided
at another facility.

INTERSECTION OF FINANCE AND QUALITY

The question of when to prioritize a costly investment in quality is commonplace in rural healthcare. Any hospital that is not
strong financially will struggle to meet high quality standards,

and a hospital that delivers poor quality care will likely lose patient volume—which, in turn, will negatively affect revenue. This downward spiral will eventually batter even the strongest balance sheet.

While the push and pull of quality and finance is a nearly universal struggle, it is especially difficult in rural facilities where the finances are almost always strained and everyone seems to know the patients. Failure to provide quality care to someone certainly has an impact on that patient, their friends, and their family, but insufficient finances can endanger the entire enterprise.

Many of the actions and expenses associated with quality care can cost an organization money without directly yielding a positive financial return. For example, setting up an acute stroke program with rapid response requires several components such as a telehealth connection to a comprehensive stroke center and ready access to expensive clot-busting drugs. Staff must train to maintain competencies in stroke care to act quickly. A well-managed rural ED can have excellent outcomes for its stroke patients. Unfortunately, as is frequently the case at rural facilities, the cost of readiness is rarely covered by volume. Hospitals can invest thousands of dollars into equipment and training for very few ED patients. Stroke patients who require acute treatment such as clot-busting drugs or thrombolytic surgery will likely only get the diagnosis and start their treatment at a rural facility; tertiary hospitals will assume most of their care responsibilities—and revenues.

The value of successful stroke outcomes is incalculable to a rural hospital's leaders—potentially more valuable than the billed services. A stroke patient who walks around town and tells everyone about the excellent care they received at the local hospital can reinforce a staff's sense of pride, too. On the other hand, negative word of mouth about a bad patient outcome can quickly tarnish a hospital's reputation in a small town. Several great patient outcomes are required to counter a single bad one.

Example: Diabetes Quality vs. Finance

Staff and the community can be very sensitive to the prioritization of financial success over patient outcomes. The slightest indication that a leader is willing to sacrifice quality to improve the bottom line can devastate staff confidence and community trust. Rural health leaders who are aware of this pitfall couch their communications to staff and community in a way that emphasizes the importance of quality care to the patient.

Diabetes provides a good example of how quality and finance can be at odds with one another. Imagine two different approaches that health systems can take to address the disease. One focuses on aggressive treatments, which are reimbursed, and the other is targeted toward the prevention of the progression of the disease.

Aggressive treatment can include toe and leg amputations or services like hyperbaric treatment to treat neuropathic wounds. Both can be effective once the disease has advanced to a point that calls for significant intervention, and both are reimbursed through most insurance plans. Leaders eying the bottom line likely favor investments in diabetic wound treatment services that can produce positive financial returns. They see greater volume in wound treatment and amputation services as a success.

However, leaders who are focused on preventing the progression of diabetes promote public education, early diagnosis, exercise, and programs to ensure that patients receive their medications. These leaders see greater volume in wound treatment and amputation services as a failure.

Leaders at both organizations can speak to the community about their outstanding diabetes centers. Without experiencing both an income-centered and a quality out-come–centered organization, it is difficult for most patients with diabetes to know which is better for them—until they need their care.

Today, the US healthcare system is in a transition period from paying for volume (by doing procedures) to incentivizing for value (by preventing disease progression). Healthcare leaders must strike a careful balance during this time of transition. It's like having one foot in a canoe and the other nailed to the dock. The yin and yang aspects of quality and financial viability must be acknowledged. As illustrated in the diabetes care sidebar, volume and value are opposites that exist together in today's healthcare system, and it is not easy to manage them.

The way healthcare organizations are reimbursed today encourages institutions to use complex care, or volume, to treat disease. In general, the more complex the treatment, the greater the reimbursement. Far less funding goes toward preventing the progression of disease, or value. The organization that wants to rely on obtaining quality outcomes and preventing disease may not be able to do so in a way that is financially sustainable until the US healthcare system moves further into value.

There is a common saying among not-for-profit healthcare organizations: "No margin, no mission." But the reverse also is true: "No mission, no margin." If discussions in the C-suite or boardroom are driven primarily by financial success or instead by quality outcomes, long-term survival will be challenging for the organization. Leaders must respect both finance and quality (volume and value) and be able to articulate the importance of each to their organization.

PERCEPTION OF QUALITY

The mere perception of quality care should never be prioritized above or even considered equal to the achievement of quality care. Frequently, though, the perception of the patients and family members who visit the facility serves as the proxy for quality. Overall quality is difficult for people outside of healthcare to accurately judge, but everyone can see if the floors are clean, the décor is fresh, the counters are clear, and the food is properly prepared. Granted, it is far more important for caregivers to wash their hands properly, but to the patient, an important indicator of infection control is how clean and organized the staff and facility appear. Stains on blankets may not cause infection, but people will nevertheless perceive them as "dirty." Likewise, leaders who encourage staff to maintain a professional appearance promote a positive first impression.

Clean floors and great food will not make up for high infection rates or poor outcomes. But attention to the things that are perceived as quality can help convince patients that the organization is professional and cares about them.

POINTS OF REFLECTION

- What are the primary quality metrics at your organization? Do they reflect the true quality of care? What are the trends in quality scores?

- Are most leadership discussions centered on finance or quality? What is the impact of that emphasis on the organization?

- Who is responsible for quality: Leaders? Clinicians? The board?

- How can you ensure that everyone sees quality as their job?
- Do people in the community believe they receive high-quality healthcare? How do you know that?

REFERENCE

Casey, M., I. Moscovice, J. Klingner, and S. Prasad. 2012. "Reference Flex Monitoring Team Policy Brief #25: Relevant Quality Measures for Critical Access Hospitals." *Flex Monitoring Team*. Accessed Oct. 12, 2022. www.flexmonitoring.org/publication/relevant-quality-measures-cahs-policy-brief-25.

CHAPTER 3

Finances and Funding

Tim Putnam, DHA, MBA, FACHE, and Nikki King, DHA

It is hard to find another sector that matches the complexity of funding streams in healthcare. The fact that a third party rather than the consumer typically pays for services adds to the complexity. Factor in the additional creative funding mechanisms to keep rural organizations afloat, and it is easy to understand why the rural healthcare business model is so confusing. The best a leader can do is build expertise on the funding that flows to and through one's organization.

THE UNIQUE HEALTHCARE MARKET

There are several reasons why the current healthcare system does not align with the typical financial reimbursement business model.

- As noted, consumers usually do not pay in full for the services they receive. Rather, the insurer pays most of the cost.
- Consumers do not always choose the services they receive or their providers. Physicians and other clinicians make many of those decisions. These highly skilled professionals

are unique in the US free market system. Other sectors have analysts, consultants, and counselors, but none have the authority or levels of licensure of physicians.

- Medicare and Medicaid set the prices they will pay. Their rates must be accepted, even when they are far below the cost of the service.

COMPLEXITY OF BILLING AND COLLECTION

Healthcare billing has grown exponentially more intricate over the years. There are several factors contributing to the growth.

Medicare has expanded to include various Medicare Advantage plans. Likewise, Medicaid in many states has a variety of plans and payment models. Insurance companies offer modified plans to fit the needs of employers. Healthcare exchanges add to the mix. Not long ago, Medicare, Medicaid, and a couple of major insurance companies made most payments in rural communities. Today, it is not uncommon to have contracts with more than 50 insurers.

In addition, physicians who are not in a plan are "out of network," and their services are not covered, or are covered at a lower rate. Each local physician or group must sign an agreement with every carrier or risk being out of network, which leads to surprise billing and unhappy customers/patients.

Small rural facilities have little leverage when negotiating payments with multibillion-dollar insurance corporations, but they don't like to be excluded from any plan, either. That would cause patients to leave the community for care—and payments for commercially insured patients are necessary to offset the losses from Medicare, Medicaid, charity care, and bad debt.

The billing process is cumbersome, and formatting claims, correcting bills, and dealing with denials is tedious work. But if a good process is not in place, slow payment and outright refusals are likely. Unfortunately, finding staff in rural areas who have mastered these special functions can be difficult.

RURAL DESIGNATIONS

The Centers for Medicare & Medicaid Services (CMS) assigns specific designations for rural clinics and hospitals.

- **Sole community hospitals** have 50 or fewer beds and are 35 miles from another hospital.
- **Critical access hospitals (CAHs)** have 25 or fewer beds and are 35 miles from another hospital or have a state waiver or designation that identifies them as critical to the area they serve.
- **Medicare-dependent hospitals** have fewer than 100 beds with a Medicare patient volume of more than 60 percent of their inpatient days; their closure might hurt the local Medicare population.
- **Rural health clinics (RHCs)** operate in areas that are designated as medically underserved or health professional shortage areas.
- **Federally qualified health centers (FQHCs)** must operate independently in a low-income underserved area or for a medically underserved population and have robust offerings in primary care, laboratory, dental, obstetrics, behavioral health, and other services as needed by their population.

Each designation comes with specific rules and funding requirements to augment traditional patient funding sources. Were it not for these designations, the services in many rural areas would be diminished significantly.

Traditional payments based on patient severity and volume have disproportionately caused rural health providers to struggle financially. They may have high patient demand, but they exist in communities that are too small for economies of scale. As a result, the Health Resources and Service Administration (HRSA) designates many rural areas as shortage areas. The two main designations are health professional shortage area (HPSA) and medically underserved area/population (MUA/MUP).

Significant benefits and resources are available in HPSA and MUA/MUP regions. One key benefit is the ability to operate a clinic that receives special cost-based funding specifically in an FQHC or RHC model. FQHCs can operate either in urban or rural settings (the largest FQHCs serve urban underserved markets), while RHCs only operate in rural areas. These models were created to serve primarily low-income and Medicare patients in need of preventative and chronic care. As such, the clinics do not offer inpatient care and surgery services. Both models offer access to grant funding and other resources.

- **Drug pricing.** HRSA's 340B Drug Pricing Program provides outpatient drugs at discounted prices for low-income patients. The funding structure is convoluted. Nevertheless, it can yield benefits for both the patient and the provider even as large and influential pharmaceutical companies frequently challenge it.

- **Provider recruitment.** Medical student loan repayment programs are generally tied to the HPSA or MUA designation, but once FQHCs and RHCs meet the HPSA or MUA designation requirement, they can readily move through the programs' steps. In the complex world of provider recruitment, speed can make the difference between a recruiting success and a failure.

- **Network of similar clinics.** The National Association of Community Health Centers (NACHC) and the National Association of Rural Health Clinics (NARHC) help FQHCs and RHCs share ideas, challenges, and resources. FQHCs and RHCs operate under very specific rules, regulations, and limitations, so there is a lot of value in working together and sharing information. A collective voice gives greater assurance that the healthcare issues of the underserved will be heard by policymakers.

Rural Health Clinics

The RHC model is intended to increase access to primary care services for patients in rural communities. An RHC must have at least a nurse practitioner (NP) or physician assistant (PA). The NP or PA must be at the clinic more than half the time and provide services such as visits to patients' homes and assisted living facilities.

RHCs are reimbursed for medically necessary primary health services and qualified preventive health services furnished by an RHC practitioner. These payments are based on CMS All Inclusive Rate (AIR) methodology and are subject to a maximum payment per visit and annual reconciliation. Even though payments are based on AIR methodology, the Part B deductible and coinsurance for Medicare patients is still 20 percent of reasonable and customary charges except for certain services such as outpatient mental health care. For preventative services, Medicare pays 100 percent of the costs. Because RHCs get one reimbursement rate regardless of services provided through Medicare and Medicaid, preventative care gets a boost because checkups are as financially attractive as intensive services that typically bill at a higher rate. In addition, the cost-based billing model creates an excellent environment for mental health providers who excel at treatments for groups, thereby maximizing reimbursement without incurring the loss of quality of care.

RHCs can operate within a hospital or other healthcare organization. Changing an existing provider practice into an RHC already within an organization can yield substantial financial benefits for the entire organization without tremendous change for the patients or staff.

Federally Qualified Health Centers

Like RHCs, FQHCs receive cost-based reimbursement from Medicare. FQHCs also may have financial advantages such as exclusive grant funding to help ensure long-term success.

FQHCs deal with more requirements and oversight than RHCs. In exchange, the FQHC model has more flexibility to meet a community's specific health needs. FQHCs must provide access to specialty services such as mental health, dental, and ophthalmological care and meet requirements for services such as transportation and translation. They must be nonprofit corporations, and more than half of their board members must have been patients of the center. The scope, patient leadership, and flexibility to meet the health needs of a community make the FQHC model worth consideration when evaluating options to make healthcare delivery viable in a small community.

One barrier for FQHCs is that they cannot be owned by another entity. They must stand independent. When a hospital and an FQHC are in the same rural community, two results may arise—one negative and one positive —if they operate under one corporate umbrella.

1. **Competition.** Resources are limited in small communities, so a competing FQHC and hospital will vie for the same limited pool of staff and patients. Vicious competition can easily weaken both entities.

2. **Lifeboat.** Should either the hospital or FQHC fail, one entity will remain to provide care in the region and possibly absorb staff. Too often, small towns are left with no healthcare provider with the closure of their only hospital or clinic.

MAIN INCOME SOURCES

Government (Medicare and Medicaid)

Many rural health facilities are funded based on the cost of delivering care for Medicare and, occasionally, Medicaid patients. Given the low volumes, the cost-based method pays more fairly for the costs of delivering care in remote areas. However, many policymakers and bureaucrats believe the cost-based approach encourages waste and unnecessarily increases the cost of healthcare, and therefore they frequently raise questions about these programs.

At first glance, a cost-based approach seems to be an easy way to financial success. CAHs, for example, are paid at 101 percent of costs, so it appears that they can make a profit on every Medicare patient. However, necessary expenses such as legal fees and marketing expenses that are not tied directly to care cannot be considered as costs, so the 101 percent is effectively reduced to less than the actual cost of delivering care for most facilities. This and other government cuts to the program guarantee a loss on Medicare patients of around 5 percent for most CAH facilities; without supplemental cost-based support, that loss would likely exceed 20 percent. The cost-based funding programs are far better than the traditional payments, but still do not provide sufficient funding for the organization to replace outdated equipment, keep up with salary increases, or generally thrive.

State-funded Medicaid programs rarely cover the cost of the delivery of care. It is not uncommon for the reimbursement shortfall in rural facilities to exceed 20 percent. Many states have expanded Medicaid payments through the Affordable Care Act. Although Medicaid does not cover the entire cost of care, healthcare organizations in expansion states have seen a significant reduction in bad debt from Medicaid patient care.

Commercial Insurance

Usually, the only income source that covers more than the cost of delivering care is commercial insurance. Organizations with few patients who are commercially insured will struggle to survive without some type of supplemental funding. Also, with the growing complexity of the commercial insurance system, rural facilities that don't have the resources to efficiently bill, audit, and collect will struggle to keep their commercial patient base.

High-Deductible Health Plans

The rise of high-deductible healthcare coverage has had a disproportionately negative impact on rural healthcare providers. When a patient has a $10,000 deductible on a $100,000 bill for major surgery at an urban facility, the hospital can take the loss of the $10,000 if the patient is unable to pay because it will still receive $90,000 from the insurer. However, rural facilities don't typically perform $100,000 surgeries. They focus on primary care and lower-cost procedures, and "expensive" care may cost $5,000. The inability to collect this cost from patients with high-deductible plans results in a high percentage of bad debt.

Charity Care and Bad Debt

Every hospital provides services that are completely unreimbursed under some sort of charity care policy that reduces or relieves the cost of care for patients who are unable to pay. There is also the bad debt write-off that occurs when a bill is not paid. These issues create difficult choices for rural healthcare leaders working with slim or negative margins.

Attempting to collect from patients who are unwilling to pay can be especially problematic in a small town. Filling the local courts with legal action to collect payment for services is likely to create a lot of local dissent, while failure to collect payment can lead to financial ruin. A careful balance must be developed with clear standards. Leaders must be able to stand up in a community and explain the need for a collection policy. The board of directors is a good resource to help judge the fairness of the hospital's collection policy and charity care.

POPULATION-BASED PAYMENT

Funding for healthcare is trending toward population health efforts—the transition from paying for volume (incentivizing quantity of care) to paying for value (incentivizing quality of care). While it makes sense that keeping a person healthy can be beneficial to the population as well as the overall cost of the healthcare system, the approach runs counter to the rescue mindset of healthcare. We know the people whose illnesses we cure, but the lives saved through clean water, vaccinations, and annual wellness visit initiatives are generally anonymous.

Rural healthcare systems are well positioned to lead in the march from volume to value for several reasons:

1. Generally, local health providers hold the health of their communities exceptionally close to their hearts. Typically, they emphasize "improving the health of the community" rather than "returning an 8 percent total margin annually."

2. Rural hospitals are, by necessity, more focused on basic preventative work such as screenings and wellness than on expensive complex medical and surgical treatments than bigger urban hospitals are.

3. The chief of staff at a rural hospital is more likely to be a primary care physician than a spine or trauma surgeon. Therefore, the medical staff is less likely to be

intent on acquiring sophisticated equipment to perform expensive procedures. High-end treatments are important, but when a multimillion-dollar investment is made in new technology, the conversation in the boardroom is more likely to be centered on how to drive volume to that technology rather than how to prevent the disease altogether.

4. Many of the moves forward in population health are connected to the social determinants of health, which the World Health Organization identifies as "the conditions in which people are born, grow, live, work and age" (2008, p. 1). Given the interconnectedness of small towns, it is easier for health, business, religious, and civic leaders to work together for the common good. Heck, they are all at the football game on Friday anyway. This gives them something to talk about at halftime.

5. Population health can be best measured in a total population. A large urban health system generally serves only a small fraction of a city's population. In a rural area, most people will have at least some interaction with their local hospital. This means that the benefits of wellness and value-based programs can be more easily and directly quantified.

The move to a value-based payment structure is moving at a glacial pace. It is inevitable, though, as more funding becomes directed more toward value than volume. Hospitals that rely on volume will struggle to survive.

FUNDING SOURCES

As farmers say, "It ain't about farming." In the 1980s, many good farmers lost their farms when they didn't keep up with changes in government payment policies. Likewise, providing great care alone will not allow today's rural healthcare system to thrive. Payment models do not provide enough funds to cover the cost of care delivered or the cost of readiness to handle a healthcare crisis when it arises. Rural healthcare leaders must keep other important income sources top-of-mind.

Local Taxes

County, city, and special tax district entities offer some funding that varies from nothing much to sizable amounts that can supplement patient revenue and allow a rural hospital to survive or even thrive. These funds come at the will of the people when they approve tax levies and usually have strings attached such as specific appointments to the board, sunshine laws, and requirements for particular services.

Healthcare leaders must be politically savvy and engaged in the process of regularly justifying the public funding they receive. It is best to get ahead of the question *Just what are they doing with our tax money?* This question will arise from elected officials, media, and the public at large regardless of the largesse. Explaining how the funds help the public should be a regular part of a communications plan. Rural health leaders need to be prepared with data and always have answers in their pocket.

Funding does not always come directly from taxes, and it varies from state to state. Frequently, these funds are earmarked by policymakers for specific programs or partnerships, which healthcare organizations can tap into. Networking with governmental connections in Congress and state legislatures can help to identify these additional funding streams. The Federal Office of Rural Health Policy of the US Department of Health and Human Services (www. hrsa.gov/about/organization/bureaus/forhp) analyzes the possible effects of policy on rural communities and provides grant funding at the state and local levels.

Grants

Opinions on grant funding in healthcare are varied and strongly held. They range from avoiding them at all costs to pursuing every possible dollar.

The "avoid" group voices several concerns.

- Requirements such as compliance with statutes, laws, regulations, and other conditions are onerous. Failure to comply can mean everything from forfeiture of the grant to significant civil or criminal penalties, and compliance can be overwhelming. Just the threat of criminal penalties is enough to kill a grant discussion at a leadership team meeting. *I don't look good in orange. Next topic.*

- Grant writing is a special skill; preparation takes a lot of time. *We are just so busy and will not get approved anyway.*

- The funds are very specific in their use and time frame. For example, the grant may only support a new program targeted to increase breastfeeding by new moms with an income lower than the local poverty level for the next two years. *Can the funds be used to supplement our current lactation program with some modifications, or does it have to be a completely new program? If we hire staff, what do we do when the grant funds run out?*

A lot of good rural healthcare systems miss the opportunity for grant funds that would support important programs due to the concerns raised by the "avoid" group. However, when the "pursue" group seeks to supplement operations with any available grant funding, several problems may arise.

- When the grants are specific in time and scope, the good programs they support eventually are canceled, and that leaves the community wondering why. This can erode the trust and the perceived dependability of the organization.

- Staff know their jobs are not secure even if outcomes are great. Where job options are limited, people cannot easily flow into another department or organization. Again, this can erode community confidence.

- The organization may be distracted from its mission. If the biggest substance abuse issue in the region is methamphetamines but the available grants target opioids, accepting an opioid reduction grant makes the organization look out of touch with the real issues in the community.

The answer to the avoid/pursue grant conundrum is likely somewhere in the middle. Grants are never "free money" that comes without strings or accountability. Organizations should not neglect grant funding that matches their goals. They need to answer some basic questions: *Does this grant help drive our mission? What will happen to the program, patients, and staff at the end of the grant funding cycle? How do we communicate the benefits and limitations of this grant-funded program?*

Foundation Fundraising

Charitable funds in a small community need to be considered differently than other funding sources. Rarely can charities alone make a noticeable difference in the organization's financial health. If a rural hospital in a town of 10,000 people has an annual operating budget of $45 million, it costs more than $5,000 an hour to run the hospital. When the hospital foundation hosts its annual gala or another major fundraising event, it can bring in $20,000 in donations or basically enough to fund the hospital for the hours of the event. An important value-add, however, comes in gathering the community together to hear heartwarming stories from patients and caregivers. Those can serve the hospital better than any of the funds raised.

Donations from individuals and groups can be an outstanding way to connect people to their local hospital. When someone makes a single donation, it can be a great step toward a feeling of ownership of the hospital. Leaders need to see the value in the "my hospital" concept and understand that ownership can create an army of people who believe in what the organization does and will help it succeed.

For example, if the staff would like one of the rooms in the emergency department (ED) to be better equipped for pediatric care, it can be an easy ask for the foundation to encourage local school kids to do a penny drive to fund the necessary equipment and modifications. The drive can include nurses or doctors talking to the kids about how the ED is a place for healing from accidents and medical emergencies, kids creating art to be displayed in the children's room, "their room," and tours upon completion to publicly thank the children for their contributions. Even if the effort does not amount to a lot of money, it brings together staff and community to create invaluable goodwill for *their* hospital today and a new generation of supporters for the future.

REFLECTION POINTS

- How much of your organization's funding comes from governmental payers? Do these payers cover all the costs of providing care for the patients they cover?

- Which model—CAH, FQHC, or RHC—would create the strongest financial situation for your organization given the current patient base?

- What forms of nonpatient revenue does your organization receive? Have opportunities to increase these sources of funding been maximized?

- What efforts has your organization made to move to population health? From a volume to value of care approach?

REFERENCE

World Health Organization. 2008. "Closing the Gap in a Generation: Health Equity Through Action on the Social Determinants of Health." Accessed February 7, 2023. www.who.int/publications/i/item/WHO-IER-CSDH-08.1.

CHAPTER 4

Recruiting, Developing, and Retaining Talent

Tim Putnam, DHA, MBA, FACHE

TALENTED AND DEDICATED people make the difference between high-performing and low-performing organizations. Having a great team to rely on can make the hard work of rural leadership so much more enjoyable, but building such a team is itself hard work. It requires attracting capable people who want to be part of a small community (recruitment), creating an environment where they can thrive (development), and keeping them engaged (retention).

Rural life presents distinct benefits over urban life, and yet it can be a hard sell. It is rare to find a rural community with enough physicians, nurse practitioners, or physician assistants. It is also quite common to see a community's health needs assessment with "access to care" listed high among the main concerns.

Not everyone will thrive in a rural environment, so it is important to identify those who can. However, once the right people are on board, the important work has just begun. Keeping them engaged can be a difficult but crucial endeavor. Tenure is particularly valuable in small communities where trust is not easily earned. It can take years for newcomers to feel welcome. Nevertheless, commitment to their personal and professional growth should be a priority of any rural organization to ensure its future for years to come.

FINDING A GOOD FIT

Any recruitment effort should consider whether a candidate will fit nicely into the community. This is especially true in small towns, where the presence or absence of fit can mean the difference between someone staying for six months or six decades. Individuals may have the skills to do the job and help the organization, but if they or their family cannot fit into the community outside of the work environment, they will not last long. And many rural communities, to their detriment, have a limited level of tolerance for newcomers or people with differing beliefs and practices.

Federal programs like J-1 and H-1B visas, which allow foreign nationals to live and work in the United States temporarily, and the US National Health Service Corps can greatly expand the number of physician candidates interested in working in a rural area. With physicians commonly exiting their residencies with medical school debts in the six figures, government funding programs that pay large portions of their debt to work in medically underserved areas are a resource that can support rural recruitment efforts. Likewise, visa programs can allow some international medical graduates to stay in the United States while working in underserved areas.

These programs and their incentives can provide a lot of help in finding physicians, but recruiting for community fit is still important. If a physician is *willing* but not *wanting* to be there, patients and staff will quickly figure that out. A revolving door of physicians leaving after they have paid off their loans or met their visa requirements will only lead to a lack of continuity that can erode patient trust in a hospital.

Common Rural Practitioner Profiles

Rural healthcare leaders must be able to determine what motivates someone to want to work in a small community more than anywhere else. Motivations differ for each individual, just as the needs of each organization differ. Most important, motivations and needs should match. The following categories provide a few helpful examples of potential practitioners who may—or may not—prove to be a good fit.

The Local Kid

. . . is returning home (or a place like home) to be close to family, friends, or a way of life they enjoy.

They understand the local culture and may have an established support system in the area. This is the ideal situation for building trust with patients and creating a long-term clinical practice. Frequently, their return occurs after some life event like marriage or the arrival of children. Rural healthcare leaders need to stay connected with ex-pats wherever they go to practice, and then make sure they know they are welcome to come back home.

The Work Visa Doctor

. . . received medical training outside the United States.

They may have practiced in another country and were matched into a US residency. To remain stateside, they may choose to relocate to an urban place after practicing under a J-1 or H-1B work visa in an underserved (e.g., rural) setting for a few years. Many physicians work the required three years and build a life and practice in the area, while many others do their time grudgingly, then leave. It is difficult to discern long-term intent in the interview process, but worth the effort.

The Baggage-Handler

. . . comes with personal or professional baggage.

Getting a complete picture here during recruitment can be difficult when the previous employer is unwilling or unable, on the advice of counsel, to share details. There can be a history of substance abuse, inappropriate workplace behavior, compromised integrity, or an explosive temper. They typically do not last more than a year or two in any one place, eventually moving out to underserved rural communities that are desperate to hire providers. The choice between having a potential troublemaker or no provider at all can be complicated, given the fact that an accurate and complete history can be difficult to uncover.

The Money-Motivated Doctor

. . . is driven by financial gain and sees patients as the means to an end.

They generally provide quality care and have high customer satisfaction because those attributes drive revenue. In a shortage of providers, the economic principle of supply and demand comes into play, and these people can be attracted to a financial premium. When rural hospitals accommodate this request, they may find it unsustainable. With motivation narrowly focused on compensation, this person continually lobbies for additional increases and ways to charge more to patients while also seeking better compensation elsewhere. It can be tempting to hire this physician to fill a critical need, but healthcare leaders need to consider two concerns.

1. What will the impact be on the rest of the staff when they learn (and they will) of this person's elevated salary?

2. Some other organizations will be willing to offer more money, which will force repeated increases or the loss of the physician.

The Coaster

. . . is generally within sight of retirement but not quite ready or able to stop working.

They are confident, experienced, and frustrated by the administrative duties of medicine. They are looking for a salary to practice medicine for a few more years without a heavy patient load and with as little office responsibility as possible. They are typically dependable and happy to avoid any drama that may arise in a small medical staff, and therefore can be good hires.

The Missionary

. . . is driven by a sense of mission or purpose that is greater than self.

This motivation may come from family values, personal experiences, or religious beliefs. In any case, this person is drawn to areas with significant health disparities where they can make a difference. Rural organizations can help them extend this sense of global mission with flexible time off policies that allow them to travel for several weeks at a time rather than traditional benefits.

RECRUITMENT PRIORITIES

Recruiting is serious business. Leaders must dedicate sufficient staff time for regular contact and follow-through with promising candidates. Clear communication should be a priority so they know where they stand. It is too easy to allow everyday functions to prevail over the recruitment process, but delays in communication, glacial contract review and negotiation, or any other type of slow response can prompt a good candidate to walk away. Good candidates always have options. Moreover, distracted responses to them during the recruiting phase will create a poor setting for a future employee–employer relationship.

Technical Staff

Today's healthcare delivery requires an array of technical expertise. Essential support skills include finance, billing, computer technology, marketing, human resources, business development, and fundraising. Small communities rarely have these skill sets in abundance, which leaves health systems with the choice of recruiting people with these abilities from elsewhere, outsourcing the responsibility, or developing their own team to perform these functions.

Recruiting people with these talents presents some of the same challenges and benefits as recruiting clinical talent. However, not all technical staff members need to be on-site or directly engage with patients, so outsourcing is an option. Rural healthcare organizations that are affiliated with larger systems and their well-developed capabilities in technical specialties can have an advantage in facing this challenge, as well.

Alternatively, there is the option of finding competent service vendors if the skill cannot be found locally or easily recruited. Outsourcing can be a tough decision in a community that desperately needs skilled jobs. However, rural health systems without competent people in these essential positions will struggle to thrive.

Clinical Staff

A good portion of the next generation of nurses, technicians, and therapists may be in the organization today. Unfortunately, members

of the nonclinical staff are intimidated by the education and training requirements to become clinical professionals. In addition, this
training may not be available in small communities without local
colleges. Leaders should look for any barriers to professional development and work to remove them. There are several remedies.

- **Tuition reimbursement.** Most organizations offer
  some support for education, yet the cost frequently
  remains a barrier. Tuition reimbursement funds are good
  investments and should be reassessed regularly to ensure
  that they are sufficient to attract applicants.
- **Partnership with regional schools.** Creating appropriate
  classes in the community can be arranged with a
  regional college willing to be a partner in the endeavor if
  subsidized.
- **Inspiration to others.** Staff should know that their
  organization wants them to achieve more. Highlighting
  the accomplishments of those who have completed clinical
  skills programs and improved their lives can be a successful
  tactic for generating additional interest.

DEVELOPING THE NEXT GENERATION: AN AGRARIAN APPROACH

A far-reaching view of clinical staff development that takes a home-
grown agrarian approach can yield eventual success when the process
starts in early high school. Programs for students can vary from
simple career presentations to summer programs and intensive exposure lasting a full semester.

A solid development program requires both external and internal
support. Creative programs that bring students into the hospital
can only happen with the help of a partner/advocate at the school
system, someone to encourage student participation and help them

work through the logistics. The hospital staff also must be on board. A few staff members will not want to be bothered with teaching others, but if this attitude is pervasive, nothing positive can come from the students' exposure. Staff buy-in and ownership of next-generation training are crucial.

It is important to choose students with a genuine interest and educational capability to be healthcare professionals. Those without family members in healthcare need special attention. First-generation healthcare students may have no other exposure to programs like this to help them understand what healthcare is really like.

Students who go through a rigorous healthcare experience at a hospital typically have several revelations.

1. It's not melodramatic like "Grey's Anatomy" or "Chicago Med," which may be their only point of reference to healthcare if they don't have a family member in the profession.

2. Their local health system does a lot more than they ever realized.

3. They come out with a strong opinion about healthcare as a career. Many realize that it's not for them, which is good. This realization would come eventually; realizing it early can save years of tuition and frustration.

This agrarian approach to clinical staff development is more like investing in a new orchard or a vineyard than a garden. Results may not be seen for a decade. A common scenario is that a rural high school student gets excited about becoming a nurse or physical therapist. After completing their years of training, they want to work in a larger city where there is a neonatal intensive care unit or sports medicine program. The idea of returning to their rural roots may come years later when their children enter the picture and they start thinking that back home is a nicer place to raise a family. Leaders are well advised to stay connected with them all along their journey because it presents the possibility of adding a well-trained, long-term member to the team—someone who will have the respect of the community and serve as an example for others to follow.

While the process is a long game that requires a lot of effort and vision to develop, notable short-term benefits come with this approach, too.

- **Credibility is established.** When a student answers the question *What did you learn in school today?* with an energetic response about their experience, the credibility of the organization gets an immediate boost. An inside advocate is always helpful.
- **Immediate needs are met.** Students can fill entry-level positions such as certified nurse assistants or medical assistants, thus addressing a crucial staffing gap in a sector that is desperate for reliable workers. Frontline experiences are invaluable for these students when they apply to competitive advanced training programs.
- **The future is brightened.** A pipeline of students who want to work at their local hospital in the future fuels an optimistic outlook for the organization. The leaders can look forward to a deeper labor pool and the students' proud parents can talk about their children's plans to fill vital roles in their community.
- **Community goodwill is created.** Every parent wants their child to contribute to society, be gainfully employed, and raise their grandchildren near them. Starting teens on their path to a healthcare career means more people in the community are cheering for the local healthcare system.

PHYSICIAN RESIDENCY

There is a growing opportunity to train the next generation of physicians in rural areas. Rural residency programs can train primary care physicians in an environment where they are exposed to a wide variety of patients. In an urban setting, primary care residents may not get that degree of exposure to complex medical patients who are sent to the system's endocrinology, cardiology, or another subspecialty program.

Although there are various residency training opportunities and rotations in rural areas, one common and successful program is the 2+1 Family Medicine Residency. This partnership with an urban facility provides the first year of training to expose the resident to surgery, trauma, or subspeciality rotations that are not practical in a rural setting. The remaining two years are at the rural facility, giving the resident added continuity with patients, staff, and physicians in the area. Because many physicians end up practicing in the area where they were trained, cooperative programs like this provide an excellent way to develop the next generation of physicians in a small community. One downside is that these residency programs do not provide enough revenue to support themselves and must be subsidized.

RETAINING GOOD PEOPLE

Happiness in a small town begins with happiness in the family. Regardless of how fulfilling the work is to a newly recruited staff member, coming home to a miserable spouse or child will create a miserable existence for everyone. It can be tough for new families to move to a small town with no familial support or connections. A special effort to help recruits and their families love their new hometowns can make the difference between a long career in the community and a short stint. There are several ways to show that support.

- **Support the spouse.** A spouse may be a well-educated professional who will struggle to find a job of the same caliber in a rural community that they could find in a large city. There are only so many jobs in small towns for attorneys or engineers. Making connections with other employers in town who are recruiting professionals can help solve that dilemma. When they agree to consider and interview the spouse of a desired candidate, the response can be very favorable. Of course, there is no guarantee of a job, but just telling the candidate's spouse that a local company will give them an interview demonstrates that the community wants them both to stay there.

- **Encourage community involvement.** Helping new people become involved and learn about the community, especially in the first few months, is good practice. Options include taking them to the farmer's market, going to see a local band, inviting them to speak at a civic club, or taking them to the best place to hike or fish. Escorting them around town and introducing them to others is the most effective way to establish connections. And probably the most impactful integration tactic is an invitation to a casual meal at the boss's home.

- **Take care of the kids**. Childhood can be rough under any circumstances, but new kids in a small town with a parent in an important position can feel extra pressure. Simple conversations with parents about what can make their kids feel welcome are important. It's not enough to introduce them to children their age or force new friends on them. This can backfire if the kids they are introduced to see them as a threat. Each child will handle a new situation in their own way, and each must be allowed to ease into things at their own pace.

Small towns are wonderful places to live and raise a family, but many unique things are often hidden from "outsiders." If newcomers are to succeed and stay, it is vital to help them learn what makes the area special. How can they take part in a barbecue or Low Country boil? Where can they see all the stars in the sky? These things can't really exist in the city and are not easily experienced by visitors. You must be part of the community to understand and appreciate what a small town has to offer.

So much about successful acclimation is associated with the effort to help new people feel welcome. This should be a concerted effort by the board members if it is a new CEO, by the CEO if it is a new member of the leadership team, or by medical staff and the CEO together if it is a new physician. Having a trusted resource to make introductions, answer questions, and ease concerns can pay dividends when the new people truly become part of the community.

REFLECTION POINTS

- In 10 years, which key people will have retired or no longer be with your organization? How will they be replaced?

- What is your process to prioritize recruitment and responsiveness to candidates?

- How can you apply an agrarian approach to build the next generation of healthcare providers?

- Do you have a plan to develop internal staff into next-level positions? How successful has it been? How could you improve it?

- How open is your community to people who look, think, worship, or act differently?

- What makes your community special? How can you share these attributes when recruiting? When onboarding newcomers?

- What are some technical positions that do not require someone to be onsite daily? Could these positions be shared with another institution or outsourced?

- How would you discern whether a potential practitioner could be a good fit in your organization and community?

CHAPTER 5

Community Health Partnerships

Tim Putnam, DHA, MBA, FACHE

EVERY COMMUNITY HAS its patchwork of healthcare providers. The services of each may be limited in scope and scale, but when they forge solid working relationships and partnerships they play an effective role in advancing the health of their community.

Such working arrangements are very helpful in extending limited available resources, although establishing them can be tricky. Small towns harbor histories of competitive behavior and even old grudges. Inevitably, providers lose staff, patients, or public funding to other providers in the community. These histories are often used as excuses to treat others as the enemy. Cultivating common grounds in continuing educational efforts, a public health crisis, or an important public policy initiative to support graduate medical education training programs that all can support are ways to connect with other healthcare providers. At the very least, leaders should always communicate with each other.

Most small organizations are experiencing more financial pressures and are far less abundant than just a few decades ago. Independent physicians, dental practices, pharmacies, emergency medical services providers, and long-term care facilities are joining larger organizations to remain viable. This shift leads to less local control and leadership involvement in the community. When decisions cannot be made locally, synergistic and lasting relationships are harder to create. Still, those relationships are necessary to achieve continuity of care as patients interact with a succession of local providers.

Local disconnection is part of a nationwide problem. Even though publicly described as such, there is no US healthcare system. There are good organizations filled with talented and dedicated healthcare professionals, but they are not parts of a truly organic system. That is unfortunate. It is confusing and frustrating for the patient when their chiropractor has no access to the information that they just gave to their family physician—transitions from one provider to another can be chaotic. That's why it is important to help patients and their medical information flow effectively as possible among organizations.

Every leader has an obligation to their organization that takes precedence over collaborative arrangements. However, rural organizations cannot survive, let alone fulfill their missions without building trust-based relationships with other healthcare providers.

LOCAL HEALTHCARE SERVICES

Good healthcare leaders must recognize sources of conflict with other local organizations and find a way to work with them when it can benefit the patients and their community.

Long-Term Care Facilities

Long-term care (LTC) facilities are seeing more medically frail patients now than in years past. The growth of assisted living services and coordinated in-home care has given more options to people with less complex conditions who in the past would have been candidates for LTC. As a result, LTC facilities are dealing with residents who require more frequent interactions with acute healthcare facilities.

The best hospitals recognize this trend and work to ease the transfer of patients. Much can be done to improve this process through telehealth consults, improved monitoring, and interventions at the LTC facility. Unfortunately, financial incentives do not align with such services and collaborations. As a frequent result, the residents are just shuttled to the ED or other care facility for care. The impact of transferring a medically frail patient is not without risk. Therefore, steps should be taken to provide more care for the residents where they live at the LTC facility and reduce the number of times it is necessary to transport them to another location.

Emergency Medical Services

The capabilities of emergency medical services (EMS) have advanced dramatically in recent years. In the past, the concept of EMS was limited to "you call, we haul." Today, staffed with professional paramedics and emergency medical technicians (EMTs), EMS can provide an array of interventions at the scene and on the way to medical facilities to greatly improve the patient's condition and chance for survival.

However, the advent of highly trained professional EMTs and paramedics who complete continuing education classes and continually practice to maintain effectiveness has made the rural model of volunteer EMS more expensive. If the expectation is that 911 calls will be answered immediately with state-of-the-art technology and medical intervention, a substantial financial subsidy will be necessary to offset the limited reimbursement that rural EMS receive. Because there is just not enough 911 call volume in low-population densities to fund these services through billable charges, only three options are left.

1. EMS must be subsidized by sources such as tax revenue, grant funds, and the local healthcare system.

2. Partnerships can be developed to provide regional EMS responses. To prevent delays, this collaboration usually results in a tiered response system with volunteer first responders in personal vehicles, EMTs in ambulances, and paramedics in intercept vehicles.

3. Large service areas can be created by one EMS agency to get the patient volume necessary for financial viability. Like regional partnerships, this option can also result in long 911 response times and a tiered response system.

Emergent transfers from the local hospital to a hospital that offers a higher level of care are difficult for EMS to cover. For example, when a patient arrives at a rural hospital ED, critical care (e.g., cardiac or trauma surgery) may not be available there, so transfer to a larger facility may be required. Local EMS departments are reluctant to perform these transfers for several reasons.

- Advanced skills are needed to transport complex medical and trauma patients. It's difficult enough for paramedics to maintain skills to provide a state-of-the-art 911 response without also having to master the care required for complex medical and trauma patient transfers.

- Patient transfers to distant tertiary facilities require EMS crews to leave their 911 response areas. Where there is limited ability to call in a backup crew, an area can go uncovered until the primary crew returns.

- Transfers take time. If the receiving facility is two hours away, five or six hours can pass from the time of the call to the crew's return. Many rural EMS staff work additional jobs, and a transfer call coming in at the end of a shift can mean missing work or losing sleep before their next shift or job. Also, every delay in a transfer causes stress on the patient, family, and staff as well as the potential for less optimal outcomes.

Public Health Department

With the US health sector's ongoing transition from volume to value payment systems and an emphasis on social determinants of health (the living conditions that affect people's health and quality-of-life-risks and outcomes), local public health departments are becoming more engaged with the acute care delivery system. Unfortunately, today's acute care and public health worlds are separate in many small communities. This is in large part a result of the vastly different reimbursement systems. While hospitals are businesses, rural public health programs in small towns depend on local governmental funding, grants and other public support, all of which can be undependable.

Another collaboration challenge is the variability in the backgrounds of staff and leadership at local public health departments. The departments may be led by people with public health expertise or by clinicians whose primary interest is acute care—all competent and skilled professionals but with different areas of interest. While physicians and nurses concentrate on improving the outcomes of individuals in a community, public health professionals are more concerned about improving the health of a population and assessing a community's needs. Simply put, acute care leans toward saving lives (e.g. surgery, medicine, therapy) and public health focuses on preventing death and disease (e.g. clean water, safe food, healthy diet). It is important to recognize the difference between these two views, but both public health and acute care play vital roles in rural communities.

Independent Physicians, Dentists, Allied Healthcare Providers

Independent physicians interact with patients of the local hospital but may not be on staff or associated with it in any other way. It is vital to develop a close working relationship with these professionals. Making it easy for them to know how to access a hospital's acute care services, getting reports of their patient's care at the hospital back to them promptly, and communicating any changes in hospital services will engage all providers in the local healthcare system.

Dentists, along with chiropractors and other allied healthcare providers, exert a significant impact on the health of a community. They are potentially valuable sources of patient information, but they have limited contact with hospitals. Dentists in rural areas, for example, are typically not available 24/7, so their patients with acute needs (who, incidentally, may lack the ability to pay for dental care) end up in the local hospital's ED. In this scenario, there is precious little interaction between the provider and the hospital.

As healthcare continues to emphasize the prevention of disease in the transition from volume to value, interaction among all health professionals is crucial. Rural hospital leaders are in a position to bridge this gap by involving allied healthcare professionals in conversations whenever possible. The ability to coordinate care with these providers is relatively easy to develop in small communities, given the limited population size and frequency of interactions. However, it will take leaders with vision and the willingness to work outside of their organization's walls to pursue these vital relationships and develop a true healthcare system.

Pharmacies

National chains now make up the vast majority of pharmacies. The local store managers may have limited ability to function independently, as major decisions are generally made at the corporate level. This makes it difficult to create partnerships. Nevertheless, pharmacists are a key part of the healthcare system. Patients frequently share their recent healthcare experiences, both good and bad, in conversations with their pharmacists. A good rapport with pharmacists can help hospitals understand what is working and not working from the patient's perspective.

The federal 340b Drug Pricing Program offers another opportunity to work with local pharmacies. The program provides funding to many rural acute care providers such as critical access hospitals and federally qualified health centers. The support can be substantial and make the difference between financial viability and fiscal distress. To have an effective 340B program, hospitals must contractually engage with pharmacies where their patients fill their prescriptions. This program runs in the background and does not require any change in the interaction between patients and pharmacists. Hospitals must set up these arrangements to ensure compliance and receive financial benefits.

Like Organizations in Nearby Communities

Most likely, there is another community down the road that people will see as "the enemy." This is not surprising when their high school teams are archrivals. Maybe one community received public funding that the other wanted, or one recruited a business that both were trying to attract. Bragging rights can be a powerful motivator.

And yet there will be some local people who will sing the praises of the "vastly superior" quality of care they received as patients in the other town's hospital. Even hospital board members share stories at board meetings about their neighbor who sees a physician in the competing community and then tries to steer the strategic plan toward competing against the other community. This can lead to launching negative ad campaigns or recruiting staff from the other community. Such actions create far more animosity than any benefits. Situations in which a significant volume is pulled from one rural community to another are quite rare when the most volume is lost to urban care providers.

Working together on joint recruitment, shared services, quality initiatives, and the development of best practices can yield far more benefits than fighting over volume. Good leaders need to work through urges to compete with the neighboring town and instead engage in honest conversations that can identify opportunities where both organizations can advance the health of their communities.

REFLECTION POINTS

- Are there organizations within your community that are seen as competitors?
- What forces create the conflict between organizations?
- Do patients in your community suffer or benefit from the local competing forces?
- What programs or partnerships could you develop to increase collaboration within the community?
- What convening groups exist in your community that can help facilitate bringing organizations together?

CHAPTER 6

Relationships With Tertiary Health Systems

Tim Putnam, DHA, MBA, FACHE

IN THE 1940s and 1950s, when many of today's rural hospitals were founded, surgery was performed with steel and there were far fewer medications and treatments available to care for patients. Open heart surgery, cardiac cauterizations, polio vaccines, and dialysis either did not exist or were not yet routine. Much of the care was convalescence in large inpatient wards.

Modern medicine has evolved to include laser and robotic surgery, new physician subspecialties, and myriad diagnostics and treatments. Only high-volume centers—that is, tertiary systems, typically in urban locations—can afford the technology or provide much of that specialty care. Partnerships between rural and urban healthcare providers are vital to give rural patients the level of care they need as seamlessly as possible. In fact, critical access hospitals are required by the Centers for Medicare & Medicaid Services to have a transfer agreement with a hospital capable of delivering advanced care.

Advancing the level of care is not exclusively about the process of transferring patients to tertiary systems when necessary. It is also about the smooth transmission of their health records, test results, and other pertinent information so the tertiary system does not have to start from scratch when receiving a patient. A transfer process built on trust between organizations can ensure that the patient receives the best care possible.

The rural hospitals most likely to be successful in the future are creating solid working relationships with tertiary systems today. Too frequently, clinical teams must rush to patch together advanced care for their patients at the moment of need. Healthcare leaders must build the bridge *before* their teams and patients need to cross it. Bridges with tertiary systems must support the trust necessary for effective patient care. As explained in this chapter, rural leaders of today cannot just concern themselves with effective operations within the walls of their buildings—the burden of relationship-building falls on them.

ATTITUDES MATTER

Some tertiary healthcare leaders and clinicians look with disdain at smaller rural facilities and tout their prestige, awards, and grandeur. Their attitude is something like *We are the best and don't understand why anyone would choose to receive care in a small town.* There is very little a rural healthcare leader can do to change this view aside from continuing to put the patient first and providing the best care possible. It is tempting for rural healthcare leaders to simply not refer patients to that system, but that may not be practical. That system may have the closest trauma center, exclusive payer agreements, or a regional monopoly on the type of care the patient needs—or it may be the patient's preference.

The arrogance of others can be difficult to swallow, but sustaining an adversarial relationship doesn't serve the patients' interests. Some tertiary systems do comprehend the value of rural facilities and appreciate their role. Rural healthcare leaders can discern their attitude by listening to staff and patients who share their experiences with it.

RELATIONSHIP BUILDING

After identifying an urban tertiary system that appreciates rural hospitals, it's time for rural healthcare leaders to bring together the various parts of healthcare delivery to build a relationship.

Clinical Staff

Rural clinical teams need to be able to speak to their patients with confidence about the care they will receive at the tertiary system. To do this, they must know and trust the place that will receive their patients. Regularly sharing feedback and reviewing processes can help both sides improve care. Such practices help to identify patients who could safely stay at the rural facility if the staff were to get the additional equipment or training required to meet the specific care needs of those patients.

Making opportunities for both clinical staffs to tour or even work shifts at each place can greatly help everyone speak knowledgeably about the other's work firsthand. It's preferable to tell a patient who is about to be transferred *We've shared all your information and concerns, and I know the team at St. Elsewhere will take great care of you* rather than *We can't do anything more for you; maybe a bigger hospital can help.* When being transferred, patients are concerned, or possibly terrified. They can be greatly comforted by healthcare teams whose leaders have taught them to speak with confidence.

Executive Leadership

The trust that health systems have for each other is often built on their leaders' respect for each other. They need to nurture trust. It's easy to look at each other only as competition, but good leaders can look past that natural inclination and find the benefits of working together for the benefit of the patient.

Board

One action worth considering is an education session for the rural hospital's board of directors at the tertiary system. Making that connection expands the rural board's familiarity with the larger healthcare system and sets up potential opportunities in the future. Although a board visit can deepen a relationship, there are potential downsides.

- The tertiary system may see this connection as a first step toward the acquisition of the rural hospital. Leaders need to address this perception upfront and make sure there is no misinterpretation of the board's visit.
- Other providers in the region may see this connection between the rural hospital and the tertiary system as a competitive threat. Keeping all organizations pacified requires a delicate dance.

Clinical Specialties

Tertiary systems may offer to assign their clinical staff to support rural hospitals. Such offers can be enticing for rural leaders who have struggled to recruit and retain specialized clinicians. However, not all urban physicians will be happy to go to the rural community. If they feel they are already working at capacity, they will be reluctant to spend the "windshield time" necessary to travel to a rural community. Subspecialty physicians recount the day they fought through a snowstorm to make it to the small-town hospital, only to find that half the patients canceled—*It was just not worth the hassle.* Foul weather will indeed prevent some rural patients from keeping their appointments. Leaders need to be aware that visiting specialists will be looking for a reason to convince their superiors that staffing the clinic is wasteful. Making their time in town as efficient and enjoyable as possible is an effort well spent.

Nonclinical Staff

Information technology (IT), revenue cycle, purchasing, biomedical engineering, and other nonclinical services may not be patient-facing, but they definitely are essential to any healthcare organization. People with these skills are uncommon in small communities but readily available in larger cities; some of their functions can be performed remotely most of the time. Partnering with urban systems to share these positions virtually gives rural hospitals access to skilled people that they could never achieve otherwise.

Telehealth and Telemedicine

Telehealth between rural and urban facilities has achieved a track record with proven benefits for patient care. This tool is great to have in the toolbox if it comes from a dependable resource. For example, access to a remote neurologist who has assessed hundreds if not thousands of ischemic and hemorrhagic stroke patients can offer assurances that a diagnosis and care plan are well-informed.

It is important to understand that the success of a telehealth program is rarely based on the equipment—the people who use it must trust each other. Leaders on both sides of the technology must work to build that trust or the equipment will only take up space and gather dust. Typically, the biggest obstacle leaders face is getting clinicians to use telehealth. Monitoring utilization can identify when trust is faltering and a new direction is needed.

Programs like grand rounds and tumor boards can easily be expanded by video to connect the clinical staffs at rural and urban facilities. This tool brings benefits that reach far beyond medical updates. The added staff connections can be lifesaving when a complex patient must be transferred quickly. Establishing a solid telemedicine program is part of building a bridge before you need it.

One example of telemedicine's value in rural healthcare is the ability to connect an ambulance to remote emergency physicians by video so they can assess stroke patients. These programs may meet resistance from emergency medical technicians (EMTs), as anything a physician can do via video could be done by the EMT who is in the ambulance with the patient. However, there are benefits.

- **Trust is extended.** If the patient can see that a physician is on their care team, they will likely feel greater assurance that everything is being done to help them through a scary situation.
- **Brain power and another set of eyes are added.** A remote physician can see the patient, affirm that care is being done properly, and offer suggestions to the EMTs if they miss an assessment.
- **The caregivers can stay a step ahead.** The physician can anticipate the next part of the evaluation by seeing that the hospital's CT scanner is available to receive the patient or by starting the remote consult with a stroke neurologist at the tertiary system.

These actions help create an environment for teamwork that is difficult to develop without the use of the video connection.

Patient Transfer

In recent years, rural emergency medical services (EMS) have struggled to maintain staff for 911 responses. Rarely do they have extra personnel for transfers outside of the region. Likewise, it is difficult for the hospital to hire the EMS staff necessary to be available 24/7 for transfers that may average only one or two a day. In low-volume rural areas, the revenue generated by the service does not offset the cost of readiness.

The lack of the onsite ability to transfer critical patients results in three options:

1. **Helicopter.** Air ambulance teams can handle complex patients and transport them rapidly. There is concern that this valuable resource may be used for patients who are not critical simply due to the lack of other transport options.

2. **Regional ambulance.** This service can cover a large enough area to achieve the volume that allows the service to cover its costs.

3. **Tertiary system.** Many tertiary systems have ambulances that can go directly to rural hospitals to transfer patients.

Option 1 is costly. Charges can exceed $30,000, with private insurance paying less than one-third of the bill), and flights can be grounded by inclement weather. Options 2 and 3 are seldom available immediately and both require extended response times—sometimes several hours— because of the distance the ambulances must travel. During that time, the rural hospital staff can be overwhelmed by regular duties while caring for the complex patients awaiting transfer.

In transfers, the rural frontline staff is charged with finding an appropriate facility that will accept the patient, arranging a safe transfer process, ensuring that the medical record gets to the receiving facility, and caring for the patient until the ambulance arrives. Leaders must facilitate the process in advance by creating a transfer relationship with the receiving facility to set referral rules, including patient prioritization. Partnerships must also be established with the local EMS and regional service because they often require subsidization by the rural facility that will not be reimbursed.

Medical Records

It is not enough to transfer the patient for appropriate care—their medical information needs to go with them. If the receiving care team has limited knowledge of what happened before the patient's arrival, both patient and care team will be significantly disadvantaged. The inefficient flow of health records, test results, and history resulting from unconnected electronic health record (EHR) systems is a bane for patients with acute medical needs.

Regional health information exchanges (HIEs) assist in conveying information from one EHR system to another but vary greatly in capabilities from region to region. They enable the transfer of information but can be difficult to access if the systems are different and the users are not tech-savvy. So, the patient's current medication list or most recent blood glucose level may be in the record, but finding it when the clinician is dealing with a patient who has a time-sensitive condition is often frustrating.

EHR systems require continual maintenance, including frequent system upgrades and updates that can disrupt access to vital information. Ownership of this process cannot rest solely on the shoulders of clinicians or IT professionals. Leaders must take responsibility for managing the process.

MERGERS AND ACQUISITIONS

There are mixed results from mergers and acquisitions involving rural hospitals. There have been subsequent closures as well as expansions of services under larger systems. Strong opinions exist among rural healthcare leaders regarding the value of independence versus being in a larger healthcare system, with no consensus on the best way to provide healthcare in a small community. In any event, the trend is clearly heading toward rural hospitals and clinics becoming part of larger systems. Local boards must decide what is right and best for a specific rural organization by carefully addressing—not ignoring—the issue.

Questions to Answer

There are a few questions that boards of independent rural hospitals must address when considering merging with or being acquired by a system.

Who Will Be in Charge?

An advisory board created to provide input to the system may remain after a merger or acquisition is complete, but major decisions such as construction projects and leadership roles will be made at the system level. The advisory board may add a degree of knowledge and competence to these decisions, but the best interest of the system as a whole will drive the major decisions.

It is also important to recognize that promises may be made in good faith, but the healthcare landscape is dynamic. Ten years after a deal is made there will likely be new system leadership that may not feel bound by the promises of the previous administration.

How Will Mission Change?

An independent rural hospital typically has a mission statement that is centered on caring for the people in its community. When the hospital becomes part of a larger system, its mission changes. The system's mission could well be more effective, but the hospital's original mission disappears. Leaders must be sensitive to the ways the change may affect the staff and community.

What Additional Resources Can Be Realized?

Many merger and acquisition discussions revolve around physician recruitment and access to subspecialty care. If this added access is the primary reason for the partnership, the rural leader needs assurances that the system's physicians will provide the care. Commitments made by the system that its physicians will deliver care in locations not of their choosing may create uncomfortable situations for patients, staff, and those physicians.

Other resources of a tertiary system that can be valuable to a rural hospital include support services that are not easily obtained in a small community. Finance, IT, purchasing, human resources, billing, and marketing—just to name a few—require specialized competencies that can be handled remotely.

Who Gets the Money from the Sale?

Transactions can range from a zero-dollar sale with the system taking over the local owner's debt and assets to a check written to the county, city, district, or not-for-profit organization that owns the hospital. The funds from the sale can go to a local foundation charged with ensuring that the local healthcare mission is fulfilled. If the new ownership closes the hospital, the foundation will have seed money to develop some type of access to healthcare. Without an organization charged with this responsibility, months of confusion will reign. During that time, the local physicians, nurses, and other staff will move or take other positions.

What Are the Purchasing and Contracting Benefits?

Large systems have the benefit of expanded purchasing power. The ability to reduce the cost of supplies, products, and services can be the key to making a rural hospital function more effectively. In addition, getting higher priority in the supply chain can make the difference between receiving supplies during a market disruption and being forced to turn away patients.

Insurance contract negotiations have been an increasing challenge for rural hospitals. They are always under pressure to reduce prices or increase the discount to insurance companies with little leverage other than canceling the contract, which would leave many people in the community unable to use local healthcare services. The larger tertiary systems can often exert far more leverage in contract negotiations to secure more favorable agreements.

REFLECTION POINTS

- Which tertiary systems in your area behave competitively? Which ones are cooperative?
- What resources does your rural organization need that an urban tertiary system might be able to share?

- Does your organization monitor the patient transfer process? What are your biggest causes of delay, information transfer problems, and communication barriers?

- What patient services could be added or enhanced through telemedicine?

- If your organization is independent, what would it gain by being part of a system? What would it lose?

- How would your patients benefit if your organization became part of a system?

- If your organization is part of a system, what resources are available that are not being utilized to their potential?

CHAPTER 7

Community Messaging

Tim Putnam, DHA, MBA, FACHE

PEOPLE NEED TO have complete faith in their local hospital. To gain that faith, rural healthcare leaders can employ various ways to get important information clearly and accurately to their communities. Paid advertising, social media, public speaking, and news interviews can be effective channels for reaching patients and potential patients as well as staff and potential staff. In a small town, however, the most powerful mode is word of mouth. This chapter explores the various communication options and how they play out. The overarching theme is that the staff holds the key to any communication strategy.

THE RUMOR MILL

Rumors are part of life in a small town. In years past, before the enactment of strict patient privacy laws, lists of people admitted to the hospital were common features in community newspapers and church bulletins. The absence of those formal outlets has created a void for gossip to fill.

Today, healthcare organizations cannot address rumors that involve patient privacy or legal issues (*I heard the mayor has cancer,* or *Dr. Jones showing up drunk to work again?*). The good thing about small-town rumors is that, if handled appropriately, most can be managed quickly.

It seems that every town with a café or diner has a gathering of seniors at a corner table drinking coffee and enjoying each other's company. The conversation can revolve around the local sports team, politics, or the weather. One thing that seems common to these discussions is that there is little indecision. Topics are discussed until there is a consensus and the wisdom of the group is decided. One way to find out what a community thinks of their local hospital or doctor is to ask this group what they think. The answers can vary, depending on

- whether they have family members who work at the hospital;
- any first-hand experiences they can share in a story (possibly embellished to keep the attention of the audience); and
- their thoughts about how engaged hospital leadership is with the community and reports of interactions with the physicians, leadership team, or the board of directors.

Opinions can vary widely from *I wouldn't take a dead dog to that hospital* to *My niece is a nurse there, and it's nice how they care about you as a person*. Although not necessarily conclusive or accurate, these views can serve as a litmus test for the overall community's trust in a local healthcare provider. If that trust is lost, many people will go someplace else.

Opinions change frequently, so hospital leaders should develop a way to keep up with what is being said in local gatherings. Stopping by to say hello can produce some useful intel. If the leadership is unaware (that is, out of the loop), rumors will circulate freely and unabated. Know the access points for local gossip and you know what is being said.

There are other ways to develop local intelligence, as well.

- **Be civic-minded.** Organizations such as Kiwanis, Rotary, Lions, and the chamber of commerce can be good resources for both gathering and sharing information. Most of the people in these groups likely want to see local healthcare providers thrive. They can be strong allies. It is difficult to attend all these meetings, but getting on a speaking schedule can be a good way to maintain a regular connection.

- **When leaks happen, be honest.** When rumors are true but sensitive, the honesty rule still applies, although not at the expense of confidential issues. Honestly stating that certain issues cannot be shared due to legal or other privacy reasons may be the only option. If there is a rumor that the hospital will lay off 15 people this Friday at 4 p.m., when, in truth, the layoff will affect 12 people and happen at noon, a denial is not enough. The response must be qualified with something like *I cannot go into specifics, but here is what I can tell you about what is really happening. . . .* In a small town with long memories, simply denying or evading the truth will yield negative consequences.

- **Counter quickly.** Leaders can put down false rumors in small communities quickly if they can reach someone close to the source of the original report and counter it with accurate information. Then whoever is sharing your information is likely to share it with others because they want to be seen as in the know with the real story (*Well, I just spoke with the CEO, who told me . . .*).

STAFF AND COMMUNITY EDUCATION

Local residents typically do not understand all the workings of the hospital. Frequently, they will drive to a larger city not realizing that the local facility can perform colonoscopies, advanced imaging, or other tests and procedures.

cial media is an effective tool that allows people to quickly see what is happening and hear directly from physicians, leaders, and staff. Creating and posting concise videos can keep the people (and the entire healthcare team, as well) informed and engaged, especially during a crisis.

So, national public campaigns like cancer awareness months (see the complete calendar at www.aacr.org) can be used to highlight the organization's capabilities for diagnosis and treatment. These promotions not only get important information to the public in a way that can be easily shared among friends and family, but they also raise awareness among everyone at the facility. Imagine having a housekeeping staff that is able to talk about the latest skin cancer screening program.

LOCAL MEDIA

Rural areas have seen a significant drop in local media in the past few decades. Newspapers and radio stations have closed or cut staff to the point they can only give cursory coverage of local issues. Their role has been largely taken over by social media platforms, which is why it is essential to follow those conversations.

Where there is a local news source, it is important to have a good line of communication with it and be the go-to resource when a health story comes across the news wire. Making a local hospital physician available to talk about how to prepare for the upcoming allergy or flu season can promote them as experts and make the reporter's job easier. An established relationship with local media also can be important later when stories come out that put the hospital in a negative light.

REGIONAL AND NATIONAL MEDIA

Rural hospital leaders see the amazing work their teams do every day and naturally want them to receive the widest possible recognition. Also, the struggles of rural health will never be known if its leaders keep this knowledge to themselves. For these reasons, it is important to embrace the responsibility of working with regional and national media. News reporters outside the community may want to tell the story of rural healthcare issues to their wider audience, including government policymakers, but they need local leaders to help them understand the key points.

The following are a few important considerations regarding wide public attention:

- When articles and segments run in regional and national media, sources generally will not have control over the final product. A 30-minute interview may result in a 20-second video or a single comment, possibly taken out of context. A request can be made for final review for accuracy, and it might be honored if it does not interfere with the freedom of the press.

- Every news report has the potential to be divisive. Even a positive article about the important work rural healthcare providers do can be viewed as negative and draw criticism when it runs in a newspaper or television station that is aligned with a particularly strong political stance.

- Tension in the staff can result when one nurse, physician, or leader is highlighted over others. Reporters cannot interview everyone involved in a story; they typically are only able to quote a few. Those left out of the interviews, or others interviewed and never mentioned, can feel neglected or unvalued.

- It's always wise to be prepared for a negative local backlash from any story and have a way to give staff and the community a more complete picture than what was released in the media. Some people want no attention at all paid to the community while others want more attention for themselves. Both groups may be annoyed. Regardless, the leader must take responsibility for getting the organization's story told.

DIFFICULT AND UNPOPULAR DECISIONS

Leaders have to make many difficult decisions that will not be very popular. Some people will understand that hard choices must be made while others will be quick to ascribe the label of "evil management."

Reassignments, layoffs, and terminations are particularly personal in small towns. When people have their livelihood affected, a natural reaction is to be angry with the decision-maker regardless of the cause. In small communities, terminations become far more public than in larger communities and vengeance is much easier. Imagine a situation where a respected member of the community with a large local family does not meet the minimum performance standards or is otherwise found to be unfit for the job. Once terminated, they can quickly spread a one-sided story throughout the community. The narrative rolling through the community can be something like *After 20 years of hard work and dedication, you will no longer see Jennifer's smiling face at the hospital. She is heartbroken that the CEO chose the almighty dollar over people who care for the patients. Please keep her in your prayers.* In personnel matters, leaders will never get to tell their side of the story: that Jennifer was ineffective in her work. The challenge intensifies when Jennifer's husband is a sheriff's deputy.

The best advice to rural leaders is to not overreact—to not cry foul when they get a ticket for speeding, their child loses their starting position on the baseball team, or their spouse gets sideways glances in town. Time generally does the best job of resolving these conflicts. It is important to stand and take the inevitable pushback that comes from hard choices. In small communities, there is no place to hide. Handling such stress with grace is part of developing a reputation people will eventually respect.

AN ANGRY PUBLIC

Challengers to the mission or even the existence of the local hospital are unfortunately commonplace. Their grudges can range from mild annoyance to rage. The reasons for disgruntlement include

- how much they pay for healthcare,
- billing issues that were not resolved to their satisfaction,
- a bad healthcare experience or outcome,
- being passed over for a job or terminated,
- public cost if the hospital receives local tax revenues, and
- frustration over a not-for-profit business not paying "its share" of taxes.

Because of the multitude of frequent interactions in sparsely populated areas, antagonists find it easy to share their discontent. It is not uncommon for them to run into a member of the hospital leadership team or board of directors at the golf course, civic club, ball game, church, or family reunion . . . venues where discussing dissatisfaction is considered to be fair game.

Occasionally, these disgruntled individuals are elected community leaders; more frequently, they are just residents with grudges against the hospital or the healthcare system in general. They freely admonish or threaten hospital leaders in public venues (especially hurtful when the family is present), at public meetings, in letters to the editor, or in social media posts.

Even if one specific issue drives their animosity, naysayers frequently make broad accusations against the leadership. It is much easier to attack the bigger target of leadership than frontline caregivers. From a leader's perspective, it is far better to take a personal attack than to let it be directed toward the staff, who probably are not in a position to fend off accusations. Leaders must fully understand the concerns that are driving the detractors' dissatisfaction, and the primary way to do that is to hear them out. It is unlikely the most serious concerns will be resolved, but when people believe they are heard, they dial back on the animosity.

An effective leadership response calls for three steps:

1. Apprise the board of directors and leadership team that there is a strong dissenting voice in the community so they

are not blindsided. Also, they may know how to resolve the situation.

2. Do not provide a bigger platform. For example, if the issue is one of quality, make an extra effort to educate the staff or community on the quality efforts throughout the organization. It's always good to be able to cite examples of these efforts if quality is challenged.

3. Media and social media responses should be handled by a professional communicator who understands how to de-escalate an accusation. Trading shots with someone who will spend every waking hour trolling social media platforms can go on indefinitely. The old saying certainly applies here: *He who wrestles with a hog must expect to be splattered with filth.*

REFLECTION POINTS

- What sources, both formal and informal, exist in your town to find out about local rumors?

- Is there a path that can be used to quickly put down rumors?

- Is there a process to keep your team informed about what is happening? Is it effective?

- What are your best local media sources? Does your organization have a good relationship with them?

- Who is your organization's biggest local detractor? What is the source of their concern?

- When unpopular decisions need to be made or people are angry with a particular situation, who can best convince the locals to put down the torches and pitchforks?

CHAPTER 8

Medical Staff Relations

Tim Putnam, DHA, MBA, FACHE. and Nikki King, DHA

A POOR WORKING relationship with physicians leads to the downfall of many rural healthcare leaders. Doctors are not employees in the traditional reporting sense. They instead require a partnership based on mutual respect and understanding.

Don't bite the hand that feeds you, so the adage goes. Leaders can forget that physicians are their hospital's primary revenue generators. That doesn't mean that leaders don't provide significant value to the organization—far from it. But much of their value comes from magnifying the revenue provided by physicians.

Leaders who work best with clinical providers can clearly articulate the valuable support they provide to the staff. They must demonstrate a passion for patient care that cannot be easily questioned. All parties can work well together by sharing respect for the challenges of their particular roles. Although this chapter focuses on physicians, the discussion covers other clinicians as well, be they nurses, therapists, technicians, or others directly involved in patient care.

CLINICAL ISSUES, LEADERSHIP RESPONSES

Understanding how to work with clinicians is not innate and is rarely taught in management classes. The following sections describe the most important issues that make working with and managing physicians a unique experience.

Loyalty and Longevity

Rural healthcare leaders tend to move on after relatively short tenures in comparison to physicians, especially primary care physicians. This longevity, tied with the personal nature of their patient and family interactions, makes physicians better known and generally more trusted in the community than hospital leaders. This creates a much stronger community–caregiver connection than most leaders can ever develop.

Intense Competition

The path to medical practice is arduous, marked by years of rigorous study. Just getting into medical school requires mastery of biology, chemistry, physics, and the development of other analytical skills that must be verified by the daylong Medical College Admissions Test. Once selected from among thousands of candidates for medical school, the students complete four years of rigorous training, followed by a residency matching system (similar to draft day in professional sports) that determines the specialty they will be trained for and where they will live for the next several years of their professional training. This process produces people capable of amazing things, but also takes a personal toll. The experience is one that few other professionals can relate to.

Financial Pressure

Once physicians have completed their training, they usually find themselves at the age of 30 with hundreds of thousands of dollars in education debt. Their high school classmates who became engineers and accountants already have homes, savings, and retirement accounts. Many physicians who want to practice in rural areas may start completely altruistic but soon find themselves facing massive financial pressure. Digging out of this debt alone can be daunting.

Dedication to Patient and Profession Over Employer

Physicians take the Hippocratic Oath of ethical dedication to their patients, the profession, and those who follow in their footsteps. The oath says nothing about ensuring that their employer makes a positive monthly margin. Leaders must understand the devotion to which physicians and clinicians have to the art of medicine and the care of their patients.

Distrust of Administration

The goals of leadership and physicians frequently are unaligned. If physicians do not see their goals respected by the administration or understand how a business strategy yields benefits for their patients or themselves, they can be a great force of resistance. Given the powerful voice that rural physicians have in their communities, this resistance can curtail key administrative initiatives. Leaders who truly listen to providers and understand their perspectives can engage them in a meaningful dialogue about moving their organization forward.

Communication

It is not uncommon for poor communication to be at the core of many conflicts. The following classic story can help explain the specific challenge.

A surgeon returns from a national conference and tells the CEO that the hospital needs a $250,000 "fancy gizmo" that reduces recovery time and improves quality outcomes. *All the leading surgeons are now using it.* The CEO replies that the current capital budget cannot be modified but the fancy gizmo could be included in discussions for the next year's budget. Both seem to agree that this is a good plan.

After the meeting, the CEO makes a note to check with the CNO, CFO, and director of surgery to determine

- Accuracy of claims about the fancy gizmo
- Availability of alternatives
- Return on investment
- Cuts from next year's plan to accommodate the fancy gizmo

Meanwhile, the surgeon makes a call to the fancy gizmo sales rep and informs her that the hospital will be purchasing it. She agrees to bring in a loaner to train the staff so patient scheduling can start the next month.

In discussions between physicians and hospital leaders, clear communication with understood expectations on both sides is extremely important. It is not easy to say no to an excited surgeon who is convinced of the urgent importance of a request, but a lack of sound administrative processes can lead to a huge conflict and a lack of trust.

Physician Leadership

Typically, a chief of the medical staff (CoS) is elected by their peers to represent their interests. The authority of the CoS can vary—they can be a resource for leadership in understanding the clinician's perspective or even be a voting member of the board of directors.

By contrast, the CMO is a member of the leadership team alongside the CEO, CFO, and CNO. In small organizations, the CoS can perform many of the same functions as the CMO. It can be tempting to have the CoS function in this capacity to avoid conflict and reduce redundant salary costs. A good CoS can perform well in this type of joint role. However, a CoS who is in conflict with the administration can devastate the organization. Since they represent the voice of the medical staff, a CoS can readily tarnish a leader's reputation with the board, community, or employees. Having a CMO in place who regularly works with the leadership team can counter the impact of an adversarial CoS.

Unlike urban hospitals, few rural health organizations have physicians as CEOs. One reason could be the salary differential. Given the demand for physicians in rural areas, a move from clinical practice to the C-suite would yield a negligible or neutral effect on salary—or even a reduction. However, physician CEOs have the advantage of "walking in the shoes" of the hospital's providers and are more likely to gain support from the medical staff for administrative initiatives. This advantage can overcome a lack of traditional business experience, education, and training, especially where there is a history of medical staff dissension.

Time Off

Rural physicians have a vital need for downtime. In addition to the stresses that their urban peers experience, a couple of factors make downtime even more important to rural doctors.

- **Call demands.** Rural physicians generally experience greater demands of call and patient access than their urban peers, mainly because there are fewer physicians in a rural practice or specialty. For example, many urban hospitals have enough volume to afford laborists and pediatricians or neonatologists on site for their obstetrics units. The cost of 24/7 coverage is easier to justify at a hospital with more than 2,000 deliveries per year than at a rural hospital with fewer than 200. So, rural obstetricians, anesthesiologists, and pediatricians share call with their partners—possibly three or four days a week.

- **Patient access.** Every rural doctor has stories about patients who have approached them in public to address an affliction of the moment. The more interesting stories include some sort of garment being pulled down to expose a rash or other anomaly for "doc to take a quick look." There is little escape from the everyday demands made on a small-town doc.

Vacations, long weekends, and even medical mission trips help physicians recuperate mentally from everyday stress. Hospital leaders are wise to recognize and respect this need. It is easy to fret about what may occur when a physician is gone, like loss of volume and coverage, but larger problems with professional satisfaction will arise from not allowing time away. Unfortunately, patient scheduling issues complicate vacation planning.

Hospital leaders, on the other hand, can take vacations and call in sick without fear of missed patient appointments that can't be rescheduled anytime soon. There are comparatively few tasks that leaders must complete that cannot be delegated. Physicians are acutely aware of this disparity in responsibilities, which makes prioritizing and respecting their time off all the more important. Burnout is always a simmering danger to the physician and the organization.

Peer, Manager, and Servant?

When working with physicians, good leaders must understand what role they need to play and at what time. At different times, leaders will be

- **a peer,** working shoulder to shoulder with physicians to solve a challenge, like recruiting a provider and acclimating a new one to the community;

- **a servant,** clearing the path of obstacles that inhibit the physician's ability to work by, for example, sorting through the plethora of rules and regulations to help them figure out how they can legally do what they need to do; and

- **a manager,** directing a physician to perform mundane but required operational tasks like charting, electronic health record system training, and other compliance requirements.

All three roles are important. No good hospital leader can succeed with only one of them.

PROVING THE VALUE OF ADMINISTRATION

From a high-level view, regulatory compliance and other administrative functions are incredibly important to an ethically well-run facility. However, physicians do not relish the never-ending flow of myriad boring data points that are required to maintain compliance, nor would they understand how to complete tasks related to state licensing without adding a lot of study time to their overflowing schedules. "Operational analysis" and "Six Sigma" may be mere buzzwords to the clinical staff who nevertheless benefit most from the efficiencies these strategies realize. Leaders who step up, take ownership of these essential business strategies, and articulate their end value to the clinical team will go a long way in proving they are true partners in ensuring that patients receive the best possible care.

POWER STRUGGLES

Power struggles are unavoidable and rarely end well for hospital leaders. When physicians feel wronged or otherwise disrespected, they can exact revenge on leaders in several ways such as direct appeals to the board, other members of the medical staff, or even to the general public.

Likewise, leaders who want to show they are in charge can deny vacations, assign sub-optimal staffing, and raise questions about quality. Rural life is a fishbowl, and none of this strife goes unnoticed. Petty disagreements will turn toxic and spread if left unresolved. Leaders must do their utmost to be aware when they arise, meet the challenges head-on, and resolve them if possible. If they can't be resolved, the board and all of the senior leadership must be made aware of the conflict so they are not blindsided when it is brought to their attention.

REFLECTION POINTS

- Are there sources of tension between your organization's physicians and leadership? What can you do to reduce them?

- What opportunities exist to specifically strengthen the relationship and trust between physicians and leadership?

- Does leadership respect physicians' private time and allow enough time off? What changes could be made to improve the ability of physicians to disconnect?

CHAPTER 9

Rural Healthcare Governance

Tim Putnam, DHA, MBA, FACHE

THE ESSENTIAL WORK of boards in rural healthcare can be distilled into a simply stated concept: *Make sure the organization fulfills its mission now and in the future.* To accomplish this, the boards must successfully align the complexities of healthcare delivery with the unique dynamics of their community. This chapter is written to help boards and the leaders and staff who support them understand the role of the board, how it does its important work, and ways to improve its effectiveness.

ORGANIZATIONAL ROLES

For context, a good way to start looking at what the board should do is to identify the three main groups of people in an organization: staff, leadership, and the board. Each group plays an essential role in an organization's mission, and each role is different.

Staff

Staff must focus on the task at hand at any given time. This can mean taking the history of a patient in an exam room, clamping a bleeding artery in surgery, cleaning the floor, or making sure supplies are fully stocked and ready for the next patient—in short, daily operations. Of course, this group includes more than the clinical staff. The people working in information technology, environmental services, and maintenance (to name a few) have critical roles as well. Failure in the task at hand can lead to any number of negative results for the entire organization.

Leadership

Leaders must ensure that the staff has what it needs to meet the needs of patients. If leaders see to it that their frontline teams possess the tools, information, space, and resources to do their jobs, they have fulfilled much of their role. This includes coverage of daily issues as well as making sure needs will be met in the coming days, weeks, and months. They must also provide accurate and timely information to the board in the format the members prefer and in jargon-free language they can understand.

Board

Board members do not need to be experts in healthcare delivery. Knowledge of how to contain a bleeding artery or diagnose a complex medical patient is not required. They do, however, need to be committed to the mission. The best boards have members who care about their community and want to make sure their organization has a viable financial strategy, succession plans for the clinical and leadership teams, and a strategy in place to meet the needs of the next generation. To that end, boards must put more effort into looking forward than reviewing reports from the last quarter. Poor financial or quality outcomes cannot be ignored, but agendas must focus on the future.

Shared Responsibilities

It's worth adding that staff, leadership, and the board are responsible to each other. If members of the board can empathize with the responsibilities of leaders and the duties of the staff, they can make better decisions about the future of the entire organization. Likewise, staff who are involved in discussions about improving quality of care can bring insights for process improvements that leaders and board members may not see.

However, if the staff does not handle the task at hand, nobody from above is going to step in and do the job. Likewise, when the board dedicates time to daily management issues, the work of ensuring that the organization continues to serve the community into the future is not getting done.

BOARD TYPES—RURAL CONTEXT

Rural healthcare boards may be elected (by city, county, or district voters), advisory (to a larger system board when the hospital is part of a system), appointed (by a governmental body), or self-appointed (by the members themselves). In any governance structure, boards can be either effective or dysfunctional. All hold the potential to be successful in their work, so leaders should respect their organization's governance structure and learn how best to work with it.

Rural healthcare leaders should be sensitive to the fact that board members from the community who have no healthcare background can get lost in the jargon, acronyms, and complexity of healthcare finance. Considering the pressure involved in making decisions that will affect the quality of care that their friends and neighbors will receive, it is easy to think that healthcare board members ought to be healthcare professionals. Boards certainly benefit by having some members with healthcare experience. They can give the entire board confidence that their decisions support optimal patient care.

Diversity, dedication to the public interest, and the ability to engage in a thoughtful discussion can be just as important as experience. In fact, a board composed of only one type of background can fall into a static way of thinking where everyone steers the organization toward the same course of action. Ideally, members represent the entire community rather than local elites or healthcare experts from out of town.

Key Attributes for a Board Member

- A commitment to the future and health of the community and the patients the organization serves
- A background that reflects diversity of knowledge, skills, gender, age, and ethnicity that is representative of the community and possibly dissimilar from other board members
- A sphere of influence that is not otherwise represented on the board
- The cognitive ability to quickly assess complex issues and understand their impact on the community

---

REPLACING AND RECRUITING BOARD MEMBERS

It is more hopeful than realistic to assume that all board members will complete their terms or give sufficient notice when they need to step down. Health, family, and career changes cause members to resign from their position with little notice. These departures can be especially disruptive when the organization is facing a complex issue or crisis.

To prepare for this challenge, boards must plan on replacing one or two members each year. Just as leaders must develop succession plans for themselves and key members of their teams, boards must do the same.

The planning can be performed by a subgroup such as the governance or nominating committee. A list of potential members should reflect a variety of expertise and backgrounds. This list can then be pared down to include the top prospects in the community who may have the ability and interest in being members. Once the nominating committee approves these prospects, it is prudent to contact them for a frank discussion about board service. An initial early conversation is much easier to have when the question is *Would you consider being part of the board in the next couple of years?* than *Can you start on Thursday?*

Armed with a short list of people who are both capable and willing to serve, leaders and current board members need to keep these prospects connected to the hospital. Some tactics follow.

- **Tap into their expertise.** If the hospital is facing an issue for which they can provide an informed perspective, engage them in a short conversation to give them a feel for what it is like to interact with leadership and function as a board member.
- **Share updates.** Provide occasional updates on the latest health issues, both national and local. Social occasions can be effective venues to both share information and give current board members a chance to know the prospective members.
- **Add them to the "A" list.** Make sure they have a special invitation to fundraisers or other hospital events for the public.

If more prospective members are engaged with the organization now, the chance of finding the right fit for the board later is greater.

Special Recruitment Cases

Elected Boards

In a public election process, recruitment cannot be done directly, although some of the key attributes will still apply. By identifying people interested and willing to run for a board seat, a governance committee can help create a pool of candidates and prepare them to step into the role quickly when elected.

Local Boards in a Large Health System

Local boards for hospitals in healthcare systems generally function in an advisory capacity without the authority that boards of independent hospitals hold. Advisory boards must understand their more limited scope. However, they can help the system understand the local implications of its actions and identify missteps, so recruiting members who can appreciate and anticipate local reactions to decisions made at the system level is imperative.

ROLE OF THE CHAIR

It is natural for board members to feel that the chair should guide the action of the board and its committees, but that can easily lead to one person dominating the agenda. When one person drives all the work and others simply fall in line, the essential value of multiple perspectives is lost. Boards that represent a broad community perspective are in the best position to follow the adage that we are all smarter together than any one person can be alone.

Too frequently, chairs assume their role is to lead the board to their predetermined outcome for an issue. With a specific goal in mind, they meet with one or two other board members to plan how to move toward their goal. Later at the meeting, these looped-in members will be well-versed on the issue and be given plenty of time by the chair to express their opinion. Since the members who are out of the loop will be less prepared, they likely will have little to say. This "meeting before the meeting" plan generally gets the chair's desired result but can easily lead the organization away from what the board as a whole would decide—and likely the real needs of the community, too.

To be most beneficial to the organization, the chair's role should be to elicit input from all members and gain insights from all perspectives. The chair should function as a facilitator rather than a driver. The best way to prevent a domineering individual from becoming too powerful is to encourage routine rotation of the chair role every year or two. When board members experience different duties, they don't become complacent. Even in situations where everyone agrees that someone is an excellent chair, it is important to rotate to keep anyone from feeling like a second-class member.

A chair who truly attends to the effectiveness and efficiency of the meeting gathers input from multiple perspectives and gives each issue the appropriate amount of time for discussion. Some chairs seem to believe a successful meeting is one that ends on time and they are tempted to plow through the agenda without paying attention to the input from other members of the board. This expediency often leads to frustration among those who take their roles seriously.

A downside of the chair's role is that they may not be able to develop their own informed perspectives when they are fully engaged in eliciting the input of others—another good reason to rotate the position among members of the board.

One important rule for leaders is to never let the board chair get blindsided. Surprises can occur during any meeting, but it is imperative that the leadership team brief the chair of any known controversial issues that could foreseeably be brought before the board. Helping the chair be successful in the role can help support an effective governance process.

BOARD AS A WHOLE

In the work of the board as a whole, each member must have an equal voice and vote. It is also important that only the board as a whole can give direction to the CEO. There is always a danger that individual board members will use their influence on the CEO inappropriately. These moves can be overt and direct, or indirect and veiled. Some examples include

- a board member who manages the local bank and pitches the bank's services in virtually every discussion with the CEO;
- a board member who touts a close friend for a long-term contract with the hospital;
- a board member who makes it clear that his son or daughter deserves one of the hospital's internships; and
- a board member who pressures the CEO to give his company, a hospital vendor, favorable terms.

Leaders are put in a difficult position when a member of the board makes a "special" request for personally favorable consideration in operational matters. Such scenarios can be prevented if all board members declare their conflicts and recuse themselves from official and casual discussions where they may have a vested interest. Board members must have equal status, and this equality must be established in the board's culture. It is also advisable for the board to empower leadership to bring forward any concerns without fear of reprisal from a member.

BOARD MANAGEMENT OF LEADERS

The bane of every leadership team is a board that is too involved in day-to-day operations. The problems with board micromanagement of human resources, finance, or other operational decisions are numerous.

- Board members may feel they are experts in hospital management. The truth, of course, is that the leadership team is far more capable than the board in the delivery of healthcare, regardless of how experienced or well-educated board members are in their professions.

- Most boards have the ultimate authority to do whatever they want to do. So, when they step into operations management, the result is frequently disruptive regardless of well-meant intentions.
- Board members may understand the operational issue at hand but probably won't be able to anticipate the downstream or collateral damage their interference in operations can cause.
- Board members may undermine the leaders' managerial authority. When the board engages directly in operational decisions, the staff will see that the board lacks confidence in the leaders, which weakens their ability to lead.

Boards should be like the passengers in a limousine. They should tell the driver (the leadership team) where to go but not how to get there. They can change the destination or the driver, but they should never touch the wheel—not even when they think they know how to drive a limo.

The opposite of the micromanaging board—and equally problematic—is one that is completely hands-off and does not effectively monitor leadership. Although this may seem like a dream for the leadership team, it is vital for the organization that the board understand what leaders are doing and why. Micromanagement is like a migraine headache that blinds leaders with pain, but a hands-off board can be like cancer to the organization that goes unnoticed until it is too late to reverse the damage. Neither board style is healthy for a rural hospital, and each can be destructive.

HIRING A CEO

Probably the most important and time-consuming work for a board is the hiring of its only employee, the CEO. It's not too difficult to get applicants who appear to be qualified to fill the role. It is another thing entirely for board members to come to a consensus on the right candidate, especially if they do not frequently hire executives. The CEO hiring process may include several important steps to find the leader who will succeed in a rural community.

- **Retaining a search consultant.** A professional will be expensive to retain but can help weed out candidates who look good on paper but do not fit the role. Good search consultants will perform the initial screening of dozens of candidates and bring forward the ones who have the potential to succeed. It is important to work with a consultant who understands the needs of the organization and what it takes to fit in the community.

- **Matching the CEO's skills with the needs of the organization.** Rural organizations do not have all the skill sets or a deep enough bench to allow for partly qualified candidates. It is important to identify all the skills that a CEO must bring to complete the organization. For example, should they have especially strong quality, financial, clinical, or team-building skills? Is it a turnaround situation, or is growth the hospital's goal? How strong is the leadership team? Reviewing the strategic plan, staff surveys, or community needs assessment can help the board identify specific strengths for the CEO.

- **Interview(s).** A rural CEO needs to be comfortable with various constituencies, including the medical staff, community leaders, and frontline team. They need to grasp concepts quickly, be honest about what they do not know, and possess the gravitas required to establish credibility in the community. An interview should take a full day or two in multiple settings such as the board room, physicians' lounge, and even a local restaurant. This variety will provide different perspectives on the hospital and its community—and wear the candidates down a bit. (CEOs must put in long days, so it is wise to see how the candidates function at the end of a long, hard day.) Also, are they equally respectful to everyone they meet—board members, staff, physicians, and members of the community alike?

Contract with a Management Firm

When a board has had a bad experience with a CEO or does not want to invest the hours necessary to vet candidates for the position, it may instead decide to contract with a hospital management firm to provide a CEO. Rural boards seem to be susceptible to this choice as it removes their toughest decision, which they may be ill-equipped to handle. The consideration of hiring a management firm prompts several questions for the board to address.

- **Where is the CEO's allegiance?** How will the CEO serve two masters? When there is a conflict between the goals of the management firm and the organization, whom will the CEO support?
- **What is the firm's real track record?** Have organizations that have been with it for five or more years thrived? Survived? Closed? How often do the firm's CEOs turn over? Due diligence includes speaking with boards at facilities that have discontinued their contracted services to understand why.
- **What happens when the relationship goes poorly?** Can the organization go its separate way? Are there contracts and agreements for purchasing, maintenance, billing, and so forth linked to the firm that will force a partnership to remain after the organization no longer values it?
- **Is this a short-term or long-term solution?** Frequently, a management firm can provide the greatest value in the first

6–12 months. During that time frame, it can evaluate and put improvement processes in place for lines of business such as human resources, purchasing, billing/collection, compliance, and quality. After the first year, the value can become less apparent, but the fees charged typically will not decline.

Hiring management firms and consultants can be a great way to evaluate current processes or help an organization through a crisis. However, the board cannot outsource its responsibility of ensuring that the organization continues to serve the community. When a board uses a management firm that is unchecked in authority, longevity, and responsibility, it effectively hands over the mission of the organization. This is a sizable risk that the board must carefully weigh.

STRATEGIC PLANNING CONSIDERATIONS

Along with hiring and managing the CEO, developing and monitoring the strategic plan are two crucial functions of the board. When well executed, the strategic plan guides the board, leaders, and staff to where they want the organization to be and how to get there. It is the key to team communication and organizational priorities. It helps everyone move in the same direction or, figuratively, pull the rope together.

The plan, once in place, also represents the dreams of the board. Leadership's job is to make those dreams come true. Good strategic plans identify the destination and leadership sets the route, which is clearly communicated to the board. Boards should put processes in place to make sure they know if they are headed toward the strategic goals or are informed quickly when they veer off track.

When to Plan

When to execute a strategic plan depends on a couple of factors. If it's a struggle to make payroll each week, spending a lot of time and energy to determine where the organization will be in 10 years won't be productive until the immediate crisis is resolved.

The existing plan's timeline also must be considered. How often boards should refresh or renew the strategic plan need not be subject to a hard schedule. It needs to be done when the existing plan no longer functions for the institution. Given the dynamics of rural healthcare, this could be as little as six months if a major competitor enters the market or in the case of a major construction project that commits the organization's direction, it can be several years before an updated strategic plan is necessary.

How to Plan

There is no single set way for a board to go about strategic planning that ensures success. The approach depends on whether the board needs a refresh of the existing plan or a blank sheet. Either way, leaders can do a few things to make sure the process meets the needs of the organization.

Encourage the Board to Own the Process

In strategic planning, when the board is fully invested in the process—that is, each member gives input that is considered—it is more likely to own it and support the tactical initiatives necessary to bring the strategy to reality.

Ideally, a committee of the board with only a few members can develop and guide the process. It is helpful for the committee to report to the board regarding the prep work in the months leading up to the planning sessions.

Educate the Board

Education in healthcare delivery topics can help board members feel comfortable with not only what is happening locally but also what might occur in the healthcare sector at large. State, regional, or national educational programs are good learning opportunities;

hiring the program speakers for a session aimed exclusively at the local issues faced by an organization can be particularly fruitful (for example: how Medicaid expansion will affect the community's health and the hospital's finances).

In the education process, gathering input from current and potential partners is always worthwhile. Key partners include area businesses, civic organizations, tertiary/referral hospitals, and even competing hospitals. A listening session that begins with *Our organization is starting a strategic planning process. What can you share that will help us better fulfill our mission?* can yield some interesting responses and engage a variety of local leaders in shaping the future of healthcare in their community.

Participate in the Process

Leaders should participate in strategy discernment, but they should not facilitate or lead the discussion with their board. Facilitators from outside the organization are better suited for the task. They can ask probing questions to clarify issues. These questions might be taken as challenges to some board members, and leaders would be wise to avoid any friction with the board during this critically important process. Using outside facilitators will also allow leaders to engage in the conversation without appearing to drive it and to observe board members' reactions to issues being discussed.

Facility Design

Facility design is almost always a part of a hospital's strategic plan, as significant changes to the physical plant can take years to complete. Because of its long-term nature, the design should look beyond the needs of today and consider the future of healthcare. This view leads to the design of flexible spaces that can be adapted to changes as needed. Rural hospitals designed before the early 1980s incorporated high numbers of inpatient beds, labs with tables for a few microscopes, and emergency rooms that were just that: single rooms for the occasional emergent patients. Many rural facilities are still using facilities designed for this type of inpatient-based care, leaving leaders to continually struggle with the inflexibility of the design.

Prognosticating the future of healthcare is an inexact science. Telemedicine, remote surgery, hospital at home, genetic therapy, machine learning and artificial intelligence, shifts toward wellness, and effective data sharing are already changing rural healthcare delivery. The decades to come promise even more changes. Boards are in an ideal situation to think about such topics when they are not tied to the specifics of care delivery today.

Mergers

Should we merge with another healthcare system? That question should be part of every rural health strategic discussion. This is not to say that more rural organizations should merge into larger systems, but a strategy session is the place to discuss the option.

The question should be phrased in this way: *Would our patients be better served if we were part of a system?* Rural hospital leaders may have a vested interest in not entertaining that discussion, as a merger may mean the elimination of several local leadership positions and the board of directors. However, the question must be asked and answered in the strategy session. If there is a solid list of reasons the organization should not become part of a larger system, all on the board and leadership team should know why that is the case. The answer to the question should not be simply dismissed with *We don't want to consider it.*

IMPORTANCE OF THE BOARD'S WORK

The labor of the board of directors of rural community health organizations is difficult and has little or no financial reward. The work also can be very impactful for the community, both now and in the future. Some board members may think that because they receive little compensation, they should go unchallenged. The work is too important to accommodate that attitude. Their decisions can make the difference between whether a community's healthcare provider remains viable.

Unfortunately, few people see the work of a board of directors, as much of it takes place in closed (or unpublicized) sessions. There typically is little or no oversight to hold boards accountable for their actions—oversight from the community, the state, or other interested entities—so they can function pretty much however they please. In short, when a board is failing in its responsibility, only the members of the board can correct the course. Boards must hold frank and open discussions to determine if they are performing their duties effectively.

Whether the board is good or bad, healthcare leaders are answerable to the community they serve, and the board represents that community. If board members stay true to their mission, they can make a positive impact on the organization and the healthcare of the community.

REFLECTION POINTS

- Is most of your board's work centered on making sure the organization fulfills its mission and assuring the mission goes on in perpetuity?

- What is the usual result when a member of your board disagrees with others on an issue?

- What is the process when an individual member of your board pressures a member of your leadership team?

- Does your board represent a diversity of thought or instead suffer frequently from groupthink?

- Does your board plan for new members or instead frequently find itself in a situation where someone is needed *now*?

- In your organization, do the CEO and board chair have a solid working relationship with consistent and clear communication?

- When was the last strategic planning process? Was the development of the plan useful in creating a direction for the future?

- Is the strategic plan an active document used to guide the actions of leadership to achieve the board's vision?

CHAPTER 10

Behavioral and Addiction Care

Nikki King, DHA, and Tim Putnam, DHA, MBA, FACHE

RURAL HEALTHCARE PROVIDERS have tended to emphasize medical health far more than behavioral health. That tendency is becoming less pronounced with the advent of community needs assessments and the shift from fee-for-service to value-based models of care.

As more rural providers are now using data to identify the most impactful ways to deploy their limited resources and look for more effective ways to keep their communities healthy, they find that untreated behavioral health issues impede the ability to resolve other medical issues. These issues, in turn, can lead to costly—and largely avoidable—services. For example, a patient with untreated delusional disorder may frequently call 911 or go to the emergency department (ED) with imaginary symptoms. This can frustrate the ED team and provide little value to the patient.

ABSENCE OF RESOURCES IN RURAL COMMUNITIES

In the 1970s, media coverage and movies stoked public concern over the plight of people institutionalized with behavioral health issues. The dehumanizing conditions in many facilities and reports of patient abuse, combined with advances in outpatient psychiatric treatments, prompted public calls for mass deinstitutionalization. While advances in outpatient psychiatric medicine eventually brought new and better treatments to support many patients in the outside world, shortages of psychiatrists and psychiatric hospitals persisted. Newly discharged patients were left to their own devices— untreated and eventually reinstitutionalized in federal facilities.

In addition, state and federal policies created an unfortunate divorce of behavioral health from physical health: Starting in the 1970s, mental health records could not legally be stored in the same location as the patient's regular health records in a ruling known as 42 CFR (*Code of Federal Regulations*) Part 2. The original intent of 42 CFR Part 2 was to protect the confidentiality of mental health and substance abuse records and to prevent the unnecessary release of information that could harm the patient. However, the strict and contradictory guidance issued in this ruling created so much anxiety in medical providers that many opted to not participate in treatment at all. With the later introduction of the Health Insurance Portability and Accountability Act (HIPAA), matters got even more complicated as HIPAA and 42 CFR Part 2 often conflict with one another as to the responsibility of a treating provider in sharing patient information. In 2020, 42 CFR Part 2 was revised to include many improvements for providers and to remove direct conflict with HIPAA. However, anxiety and misunderstanding of the special rules regarding behavioral health records persisted. In this environment, only the largest medical facilities continued to offer psychiatric services, making behavioral healthcare absent in much of rural America.

With few local resources readily available to them to use in their rural communities, many medical practitioners lost sight of the association between behavioral health and physical health. Psychiatric screening in primary care and ED settings became uncommon because of the lack of referral options for treatment, poor coordination of care with outside behavioral healthcare providers, and the inability to integrate meaningful behavioral health data into the patient's electronic health record.

The lack of local access to behavioral healthcare has hampered the ability to meet the waves of opioid and methamphetamine addictions that are now commonplace throughout rural America, where people desperate to break their addictions have few choices other than inpatient treatment facilities that are far away. Tragically, even after successful treatment, patients in recovery frequently return home with no help to cope with the same challenges, people, and access to drugs that first drove them to addiction. Lacking local access to behavioral healthcare services, many patients relapse into their previous addictive behavior.

APPROACHES TO ADDICTION

Widespread substance use disorder in rural areas cannot be resolved by healthcare organizations alone. Without the resources to treat behavioral health issues, most rural health providers can do little more than perform interventions for patients after they overdose.

In addition to securing the treatment resources necessary to combat addiction, rural healthcare leaders need to address several related areas of concern.

- **Prescription practices.** Careful evaluation of prescribing practices is necessary to assure patients and their communities that the health organization they trust is not creating the problem. This is bumpy ground, as many physicians object to the oversight. Leaders must have the physician leadership support of any project to review the prescribing of controlled medications.
- **Access to naloxone.** The US Food and Drug Administration has approved public access to naloxone to reverse the impact of opioid overdoses and help a non-breathing person regain consciousness. When this treatment is readily available, lives are saved. As their communities' primary (and typically only) healthcare

providers, rural hospitals and clinics must partner with health departments, drug prevention task forces, and law enforcement agencies to ensure that naloxone is accessible, along with adequate training on how to use it.

- **Education.** Some communities face up to the problem of addiction, while others sweep it under the rug to hide the truth. To make a positive impact on the most lives, it is important to make sure the entire community fully appreciates the widespread harm that addictions cause. Because they can leverage healthcare professionals' understanding of mental health challenges and access local data, healthcare leaders are in a good position to explain the problem and its solutions.

- **Law enforcement and judicial responses.** Building a positive relationship with the criminal justice system can support a rural hospital's addictions program. If local authorities only see people with substance use disorders as criminals, those individuals cannot be treated without the threat of prosecution. Healthcare leaders, police, and legal authorities must work in unison by regularly meeting to establish an integrated approach defined by insight, education, and role clarity.

THE LINK BETWEEN BEHAVIORAL AND PHYSICAL HEALTH

A large-scale study in the late 1990s found that a history of childhood abuse and neglect often precipitated obesity later in life (Felitti et al. 1998). This study further showed that childhood trauma also predicted chronic health conditions such as substance use, hepatitis, chronic obstructive pulmonary disease, and cancer (usually preceded by increased tobacco use). These associations present special challenges in rural communities that have higher than average rates of child abuse and neglect, higher rates of suicide, and a less developed mental health safety net. Unfortunately, behavioral health treatments that can erase the pathological basis for these chronic conditions before they develop are seldom available in rural communities. These treatments may also be strongly disincentivized in current fee-for-service payment models that rural providers have historically depended on. The discovery of the linkages among childhood trauma, mental illness, and physical health emphasizes the need to establish a community network to support the lifelong physical and behavioral health of local residents.

VOLUME TO VALUE AND ACCESS TO BEHAVIORAL HEALTHCARE

Because of the lack of resources and generally poor reimbursement for behavioral healthcare, most rural organizations cannot provide all of the behavioral healthcare their communities need. Even the most mission-minded ones struggle to provide these services.

New value payment models are attempting to prioritize the healthcare spend on preventative services—including behavioral healthcare—that can decrease mortality and morbidity. There are various iterations of these models, but the idea typically revolves around payers incentivizing good patient outcomes and disincentivizing complex procedures, expensive hospital-based services, and poor health outcomes. This shift can help rural healthcare delivery. For example, in a rural area, there is likely "the" hospital, which is the only one for miles around, while an urban area is served by several hospitals. Thus, the rural hospital has more of a defined population, and any changes that can improve the health of that population can quickly become clear.

Behavioral health provides a unique opportunity for rural healthcare organizations to support their patient population and excel in value-based care by attacking the roots of chronic conditions. Even as reimbursement from government payers remains dismal, the cost of providing behavioral healthcare can be mitigated by recruiting master's-prepared therapists. When they provide their services in conjunction with primary care providers, the overall quality of care improves and the demand for locally owned primary care services increases. For example, compliance with regular health checkups improves when therapists and social workers are part of a patient's care team—with everyone working together seamlessly. Behavioral healthcare services can nicely complement established high-intensity/high-frequency programs like prenatal care and obstetrics services. Assembling such a team is feasible even in a small rural hospital because social workers are more plentiful and less costly than medical specialists such as obstetricians, they do not require on-call hours or pay, and they can have a dramatic effect on patient retention and quality outcomes improvement.

So, the good news is that behavioral healthcare services, like women's health services, can be an excellent gateway for patients of all ages into their local healthcare system. Patients who see a therapist with a rural organization and establish a relationship with a primary care provider in the same place will likely remain patients throughout their lives. They can also enjoy a higher quality of care when they have a comprehensive clinical team.

Unlike the demand for obstetrics services in rural communities, the demand for behavioral healthcare is climbing, especially in younger populations. The COVID-19 pandemic saw behavioral health–related ED visits increase by 24 percent for children aged 5–11 and 31 percent for those aged 12–17 compared with prepandemic ED visits—and all this while substance abuse and substance abuse–related deaths continued to be a leading cause of death for adults in rural communities (Leeb et al. 2020).

By packaging long-term therapy services with regular physical care through the same health system, rural facilities can leverage behavioral healthcare services to support other more margin-friendly services such as inpatient services or surgery in a mission-oriented way. Also, rural organizations can position themselves well for success in value-based reimbursement models by proactively attacking the root of the most expensive chronic diseases such as heart and lung disease.

REFLECTION POINTS

- Does your community see the clear need for access to behavioral healthcare?

- Can your organization coordinate local behavioral healthcare and medical care? If so, how is this possible in your community?

- What resources exist locally for treating addiction? Are they enough to meet the needs of your community?

- How can specific value-based or population health programs support the expansion of behavioral healthcare programs at your organization?

REFERENCES

Felitti, V. J., R. F. Anda, D. Nordenberg, D. F. Williamson, A. M. Spitz, V. Edwards, M. P. Koss, and J. S. Marks. 1998. "Relationship of Childhood Abuse and Household Dysfunction to Many of the Leading Causes of Death in Adults." *American Journal of Preventative Medicine* 14 (4): P245–48. https://doi.org/10.1016/S0749-3797(98)00017-8.

Leeb, R. T., R. H. Bitsko, L. Radhakrishnan, P. Martinez, R. Njai, and K. M. Holland. 2020. "Mental Health–Related Emergency Department Visits Among Children Aged <18 Years During the COVID-19 Pandemic—United States, January 1–October 17, 2020." *Morbidity and Mortality Weekly Report* 69 (45):1675–80. www.cdc.gov/mmwr/volumes/69/wr/mm6945a3.htm?s_cid=mm6945a3_w.

CHAPTER 11

Crisis Preparation and Response

Tim Putnam, DHA, MBA, FACHE

It seems rural healthcare facilities are always under pressure to justify their existence. Federal and state leaders with an urban background wonder *Why do we need clinics and hospitals in small communities? Can't those folks just go to the city for care?*

The answer to both questions is that the responsibilities of local hospitals and clinics go far beyond providing health services. Rural healthcare teams provide concrete proof of their value to their community when they answer the call to a local crisis. They have the responsibility to respond 24/7, which is especially important in the first few hours.

Every hospital drills several times a year for mass casualties and catastrophic events. The information in this chapter should not be interpreted as a replacement for those plans, emergency management procedures, or the incident command process. Those practices are time-tested to suit a variety of situations and help multiple agencies—principally hospitals, local law enforcement agencies, fire departments, and emergency medical services (EMS) providers—coordinate an effective response to a crisis. This chapter will highlight some of the specific topics and challenges related to preparing for and responding to a crisis in a rural area.

PREPARING FOR DISASTER

While drills are essential, the crisis that occurs will seldom be like the ones in a drill. There are simply too many variables related to the situation, timing, available staff, and so forth. Training must be taken seriously but tempered by the realization that the real thing will happen differently than anyone has ever imagined. There are just too many variables and, frequently, too few resources.

One especially helpful process is an administrative call system to handle issues that go beyond routine for frontline staff. The administrator on call during a crisis might be there only to support the recommendations from frontline staff. Staff needs to know they are supported by leadership during a crisis. Frequently, the administrator on call functions, at least initially, as the incident commander to establish a chain of command.

RESPONSES TO RURAL CRISES

Engaging Incident Command

One of the first responses to a crisis should be to engage the hospital incident command system (HCIS) developed by the Federal Emergency Management Agency (see https://training.fema.gov/emiweb/is/icsresource/). Essentially, HICS coordinates a response to a crisis that could overwhelm the organization's regular capacity. During large-scale events, HICS standardizes communication and responsibilities among responding agencies.

Too frequently, there is reluctance to engage HICS, either because people don't want to admit they can't handle a situation or they don't want anyone else to interfere with their plans. The general guidance should be: When in doubt, call it. It is always far better to be ready than to delay a response. There can be a minimal downside, even if the crisis turns out to be not as large as initially thought. Applying

HICS anytime there is the possibility of needing it can serve to prepare a team for the real thing even more effectively than a drill.

Communicating with Staff and Community

Informing the staff and community about what is happening, the local response required, and the next steps must be part of the rural hospital leader's job. A small staff can be quickly overwhelmed in a crisis. Additional people can aid in the response, especially when the crisis lasts several days.

Today's variety of communication platforms makes it easy to get information out quickly and broadly to get everyone on the same page, coordinate resources, and marshal support. For example, a video shared through social media can be useful in presenting timely, accurate, informative, and calming messages. Of course, leaders must have a vetting process in place to ensure that the information is not only speedy but also accurate and legally sharable with the public.

Also, when concerned family members arrive at the local hospital during a mass casualty event, they expect truthful answers. Establishing a source for information and communication for them to turn to allows clinical teams to do their jobs without also managing communication. Leaders must have a solid communication plan ready to go and be able to modify it as needed.

Gathering Local Support

Rural folks seem to know they need to pitch in and help when their neighbors are in desperate need. In a crisis, uncontrolled outpouring can become a hindrance, so leaders must anticipate it. They must be told how they can help. Scores of untrained people showing up to "do something" is rarely what is needed, but there are almost always some skills that can come in handy. In addition, established local leadership networks are invaluable in extreme situations that require unorthodox solutions.

Telling the Story

After a crisis has passed, hospital leaders must make sure that their team's efforts are widely known by documenting and photographing the response, including the experiences of the people affected (with their written permission, to protect privacy) and the team members who stepped up to help them. In addition, the story will help sustain the organization's culture after the events fade from memory. Reminding people of how important their local hospital is to the community can pay dividends in terms of community support for the hospital. Of course, it is important to be mindful and respectful of the tragedy and losses that have occurred.

CONSIDERATIONS FOR SPECIFIC SITUATIONS

Responding to Short-Term Crises

Storms, mass shootings, multiple-vehicle accidents, chemical spills, and so forth require a swift response. In these situations, distant regional resources will not be immediately available and will then take time to arrive. Rural institutions simply can't wait; they must be ready to flex up to meet the immediate demand. When it arrives, regional support (additional staff, patient transfers, ambulances, etc.) must be sorted out in the chaos to ensure that the local staff has what it needs. Clear communication through the incident command system is the key to this process.

When events like a train wreck or a mass shooting hit a small town, media from the region descend on the community, and the local hospital is typically called on to provide details. Reporters want to have access to patients and staff and all manner of other things that will disrupt what needs to be done. The media have an important job, and it is reasonable (and useful) to help them do it without endangering the team or patients. It may be tempting to simply try and shut them down from all access, but left undirected, reporters will undoubtedly poke around for the story. It is also tempting to prioritize the requests for information from national and state media, but long after an event, local reporters will still be around, and they will remember if they were shut out of a big story. It's good practice to consider the local reporters first.

Responding to Long-Term Crises

Disasters such as hurricanes, blizzards and ice storms, terrorist attacks, wildfires, floods, earthquakes, and so forth leave a more lasting impact on a community. They require both an immediate response and a long-range plan. Regional resources will be over-whelmed, and a federal response will take days or weeks to arrive.

The local hospital may be able to manage those first 12–24 hours, but its leaders must think ahead about how to at least manage personnel in days 2–14 of the crisis. Every member of the staff will want to step up and help initially, but they will likely be exhausted in 18 hours when the crisis is still going on. It is hard to keep key people on the bench when there is so much action taking place, but leaders need to make sure there is a team in reserve during a long-term crisis.

Plans should also include temporarily empowering people to assume additional responsibilities during the crisis. For example, frontline members of the dietary staff may need to be responsible for feeding hundreds of people who have sought out the hospital for refuge. Doing so could include procuring extra food through alternate channels, enlisting help serving meals, and handling other related duties beyond their typical scope of work. Most people are willing to step into this role, but leaders must encourage them to do so and recognize their work after the crisis is over.

Long-term crises frequently take out electrical power distribution and other utilities. The hospital may be the only place with electricity, drinkable water, and a climate-controlled environment. In these situations, leaders must be prepared to shelter the vulnerable by expanding the capabilities of the facility to house and feed people until emergency shelters can be arranged.

Responding to Extended Crises

In extended crises such as disease outbreaks, rural facilities may find themselves standing in line for resources behind bigger-market hospitals. To gain access, leaders may need to coordinate their needs with other smaller providers in the region, state, and nation who are facing the same challenges.

Even as the situation shifts, planning for the long run remains crucial in managing resources. This is difficult when caught up in a crisis, but leaders must prepare for the days ahead. If a crisis turns out to be shorter than anticipated, no critical damage is done. As the COVID-19 pandemic has demonstrated, however, if a crisis persists, the results of insufficient planning can be damaging as supplies, staffing, and other resources of the nation become increasingly stressed. Taking the time now to consider staffing and facility expansion can help lay the groundwork for necessary moves in the future. The existence of such plans can assure the staff that their organization's leadership is not just winging it.

Throughout these dynamic situations, misinformation will be rampant. Leaders should keep their healthcare team and community informed on the latest local information. Careful adherence to accuracy as much as possible without trying to predict the future will help maintain the confidence of the community.

Extended crises provide plenty of time for leaders to engage with the community. As the pandemic has illustrated, vital help may come in the form of restaurants delivering food for the healthcare team, retired clinicians returning for duty, and volunteers stepping up to staff vaccine clinics. Especially in small communities, people want to be part of the solution—but it takes creativity to find ways to meaningfully engage them.

REAL-LIFE EXAMPLES OF COMMUNITY ASSISTANCE

A Short-Term Local Crisis

When a tornado struck 30 miles away from a rural hospital, its leaders anticipated receiving only a few patients. Two other hospitals were closer to the storm area. However, the tornado had taken out a large swath of trees and power lines, forcing the more-distant hospital to become the primary receiving hospital. With tornado sirens still sounding, all available EMS crews in the region were dispatched with the hope that the injured could be reached and safely transported.

When the injured patients arrived, they had just survived a horrific event. Some had lost loved ones, homes, pets, and virtually every possession they owned. Distraught patients and families asked the staff vital questions they could not answer like *Did my family survive?*

Support from local ministers and the hospital's entire social services team made an amazing impact. People needed immediate support to face the loss of so much of what they loved. Their recovery required more support than any single rural organization's clinicians could provide

A Long-Term Regional Crisis

When an ice storm hit the region, it shut down power and made many roads impassable for days. This crisis did not involve massive injuries, but frail people were without power for their heat and oxygen systems. They did not need hospital care, but as one of the few local facilities with heat and electricity backup systems, the hospital was the place of refuge for dozens of people. This required several creative solutions.

- Large areas including physical therapy and meeting rooms were set up to house the medically vulnerable, and people from the community volunteered to watch them. When the call went out, local citizens, business owners, and the fire department donated cots, blankets, and mattresses.
- City officials gained access to the local grocery store to acquire the food necessary to feed all the people. School officials also provided food from their cafeteria.
- The dietary department had only two staff members on duty when the storm hit, and nobody else was able to make it to the hospital. The most senior member had just two months of experience but was now in charge of feeding the patients, staff, volunteers, and others being housed at the hospital. She needed to know that leadership supported her and would secure the resources she needed to accomplish her work.

Lessons Learned

These experiences with community responses to short- and long-term disasters yielded lessons that leaders can apply to future responses.

- The rural community will step up to help. These eager volunteers should be factored into plans now so that they can be deployed as effectively as possible in the future.
- Members of the hospital's team may need to go far beyond their regular duties to accomplish what is necessary. This should be communicated to them when drilling or planning for crises.

- Rural hospitals function as more than a place for healthcare delivery during a catastrophe. The organization and its leaders must be flexible and creative to serve their community's needs during a crisis.

- The trauma of a mass casualty event will affect the healthcare team's neighbors and loved ones, and staff will need to care for patients they know while members of their own family may still be in harm's way. Later, the community will relive the event as funerals take place, and years will pass before people can regain a sense of normalcy. Hospital leaders must proactively reach out to peers who have experienced a mass casualty event and are now able to provide guidance to help others face the trauma.

REFLECTION POINTS

- What was the last major crisis your community faced?

- How do staff, other response agencies, and the community feel now about your organization's response? Can they "tell the story"?

- How often is HICS drilled at your hospital? How seriously does the team take these drills?

- How involved is your community in the drill? Do local high school students take part as patients?

- Is there a good communication process in place to inform civic leaders during a crisis? Have you included local media and social media in your plans?

CHAPTER 12

Healthcare Equity: A Rural Perspective

Tim Putnam, DHA, MBA, FACHE

MOST PEOPLE SEE health equity as a big-city issue. Certainly, urban populations suffer from the effects of inequitable healthcare. However, widespread closures of rural hospitals and clinics have made it clear that rural Americans also have more limited access to providers. Mortality and life expectancy data show that shorter lifespans for rural residents are the clearest indicator of the inequity that rural healthcare leaders must address.

In general, rural citizens experience poorer health and more negative health outcomes than their urban counterparts, which has not always been the case. Before 1990, for example, there was little discernible difference between rural and urban life expectancy. In the 1990s, the statistical landscape started to change; by 2009, rural Americans were dying 24 months earlier than their urban counterparts (National Advisory Committee on Rural Health and Human Services 2015), and the gap is continuing to grow. That means 730 fewer days to spend with family, watch sunsets, and enjoy the other pleasures of life.

SHRINKING ACCESS TO CARE

Access to acute care services like obstetrics as well as home health and emergency medical services (EMS) coverage is being lost on the rural landscape. Largely gone are the days of the local independent physicians—the maze of insurance plans and compliance rules have forced many of them to join large networks. This situation typically leaves one clinic or hospital as the sole option for most of the acute care in a rural community. More frequently, there is no local care at all. This would not be so much of a problem if rural residents had access to dependable transportation and the flexibility to go an hour or two away for care, but frequently they do not. When local care is unavailable, many people go without it.

SOCIAL DETERMINANTS OF HEALTH CHALLENGES

Social determinants of health such as access to healthy food, good schools, clean air and water, local jobs, safe housing, and public transportation are just a few of the concerns negatively affecting rural residents. For example, fresh food has disappeared with the closing of many local grocery stores. Now, dollar stores and gas stations/convenience stores are common access points for food, and they emphasize processed, packaged foods over more perishable, healthful choices.

Public health services in rural areas are generally limited in size and scope. It is not uncommon to find a part-time staff responsible for covering thousands of people and hundreds of square miles, making safety-net services for homelessness and domestic violence far less accessible. This common reality is frequently dismissed with the archaic and inaccurate belief that "eggs are cheaper in the country." Life is expensive for rural people living in poverty who lack robust social programs, public transportation, and most of the other services that are available to lower-income urban residents.

OPERATIONAL CONCERNS

For rural healthcare leaders, the operational and financial viability of the institution plays a major role in the ability to provide access to care. These challenges are rarely solved in the rural healthcare environment and must be constantly managed. And no matter how strong a rural hospital may appear to be to its community, just a few bad financial months or key resignations can send it reeling.

- **Economics.** The care and services provided at rural clinics and hospitals are not reimbursed at high enough rates to cover their costs, especially at the low volumes seen in most rural communities. During the Great Recession of 2008, many rural areas lost employers along with the commercial insurance benefits they provided to employees. This increased the already high rates of bad debt, charity care, and Medicaid, which caused rural facilities to lose money on a large portion of the care delivered. It is difficult to track how many important services like pediatrics, obstetrics, and cardiac rehab rural facilities have had to cut to remain financially viable. Undoubtedly, the loss of these services has a significant impact on the ability to access the care many people need.

- **Staffing.** In addition to recruiting clinicians who want to work in rural areas—which is not easy— health systems also must find information technology professionals, finance experts, biomedical engineers, and other technically trained individuals to provide today's healthcare. Without the availability of these skilled people, even a financially viable health system will eventually struggle to survive.

- **Regulations.** The justification that policymakers frequently give for their universal regulations (without consideration of how they will be paid for) is that rural areas should be expected to provide the same caliber of care as urban areas. In response, rural healthcare leaders echo a response similar to that voiced by pediatricians: Just as children are not small adults, rural is not small urban. If the special circumstances of the rural environment are not considered, the sad alternative is no access at all (see sidebar).

A Sensible Solution for Stroke Care

Regulations that make sense in urban areas can create insurmountable barriers in rural areas. Acute stroke care provides one example of that reality. Many states have considered legislation to require ambulances to take all potential stroke patients to the closest comprehensive stroke center, bypassing the closest hospital. This makes sense in densely populated areas where the choice is between a 5-minute ride to a community hospital or a 15-minute ride to a state-of-the-art stroke center. However, in rural areas, this regulation creates some specific problems.

- The closest stroke center may be more than an hour's drive away, resulting in the death of additional brain cells and possibly taking the patient out of the time window for many effective treatments of ischemic stroke.
- The limited service available in rural areas is further depleted when ambulances make long runs out of the service area. This situation generally requires a mutual response from other ambulance services in the region, creating long 911 response times for other patients.
- Possible stroke patients are far more frequent than actual stroke patients. Several conditions can mimic a stroke. Transferring all possible stroke patients reduces the already low volume at rural hospitals. There is also less ability for the rural hospital to develop a stroke program for non-ambulance patients because of the low volume.

Rather than mandating the transfer to a stroke center, another option is to establish a coordinated stroke response network of hospitals and EMS. Unfortunately, this is harder to put into legislative language than a simple mandate. The people who write such regulations may be well-intentioned but largely unfamiliar with the challenges in rural areas. In the room where the rules are written, there are usually few people who hear the sound of crickets at night and are attuned to real life in the country.

Without strong rural input and watchfulness, more such well-intentioned but damaging regulations will be created. Rural leaders must speak up when regulations are written. This requires active involvement in state legislative and bureaucratic processes. Following statewide organizations and associations can help identify when new regulations are pending. However, working directly with local representatives can be most helpful in averting a regulatory crisis when potentially damaging regulation is being considered.

HELPING THE MARGINALIZED

There are several at-risk groups within a small community, and each has its own set of health equity challenges that are amplified in a rural setting.

BIPOC populations—Black, indigenous, and people of color—represent 15 percent of the rural population but 30 percent of rural residents in poverty (Henning-Smith et al. 2019). These groups come up against the language barriers, social biases, and stigmas seen by similar populations across the nation while also bearing the burdens of limited access to care and other resources that all rural citizens experience. They are underrepresented in the clinical workforce, too. Leaders should actively work to involve this population when working on projects like the community needs assessment to bring forward the entire community's perspective.

Another group that faces difficulties in rural America is the LGBTQ+ population. The typical social structure in a rural area is built on families rather than relationships between unrelated individuals, and that reality can raise barriers to equitable treatment for LGBTQ+ residents who have been ostracized from their families, which, in turn, alienates people from their primary social connections. Local churches also serve as strong social connectors in rural areas, and some hold unwelcoming religious beliefs about LGBTQ+ individuals. Losing two principal social support systems can make life difficult for anyone in a small town. That loss can be especially problematic with conditions such as substance use disorder because some addiction services in rural areas are provided through faith-based organizations. Rural healthcare leaders must realize that the LGBTQ+ population may not have the resources and family support enjoyed by many others in their community.

In addition to the systemic challenges that BIPOC and LGBTQ+ patients experience just by being in those populations, there are far fewer social support resources in rural areas to address homelessness, disability, domestic abuse, and behavioral health conditions than in the city. Rural healthcare leaders need to work with other service providers in the community to find holistic solutions to inequitable care. They also must provide training to help their caregivers understand the cultural challenges that disadvantaged patients face.

TELEMEDICINE AS A TOOL TO EXTEND ACCESS

As the COVID-19 pandemic has demonstrated, video technology can reduce inequitable access to certain types of care, but only when all parties are willing and able to use it. Providers—and payers—typically prefer patients to be seen in person, but this can be a great inconvenience to many rural patients. Imagine trying to arrive in time for a 9:45 a.m. appointment at an office 70 miles away, down two-lane roads, and you must depend on a friend or relative to drive you. The logistics can be daunting. Telemedicine can eliminate the logistical challenges if adopted by more providers and paid like in-office visits. But until the acceptance is higher and reimbursement rates are similar to in-office visits, this modality will continue to be of limited help in improving equity in healthcare.

Hybrid offices with broadband service and telehealth equipment staffed by nurses and medical assistants can provide a solution to the problem of limited access. They may be located at a provider's facility or in a stand-alone location. A transportation challenge may persist but traveling 10 miles for a visit to a familiar office is preferable to traveling 60 miles to somewhere unfamiliar. As long as the payment structure makes this type of arrangement very difficult to achieve, rural leaders need to advocate for creative solutions like this to serve their patients.

HOW RURAL HEALTHCARE LEADERS ADVOCATE FOR EQUITY

The case for equity in rural healthcare has had far less attention than it deserves. Rural leaders need to raise the issue and make equity part of their personal vernacular, their organization's quality of care reports, and their overall mission. Without providing equity to all patients, can an organization give truly high-quality care? Rural leaders are in the position to convince policymakers and payers to fully recognize inequity and advocate for changes in regulations and reimbursements.

1. **Share rural equity concerns and examples.** Frequently, well-meaning urbanites will assert that they understand the difficult health issues rural Americans face, but their knowledge may be gathered from secondhand accounts or by driving through or flying over rural areas. Their concern is genuine, but there is a big difference between driving by

a prison and being incarcerated. Rural healthcare leaders must make the case for rural health equity. To start, annual reports and community needs assessments should highlight all organizational efforts to identify and rectify specific inequities. Gathering and sharing stories about rural realities are always helpful.

2. **Join with other populations who also suffer from health inequity.** Finding compatriots in the cause is important. For example, on the surface, inner-city and rural areas may not seem to have much in common, but when it comes to access to healthcare, the basic challenges are the same. Inner-city and rural healthcare leaders can make a powerful statement when standing together and advocating to the state legislature that their communities both suffer from a lack of access to care, and it must be addressed. Because the US rural population is relatively small, its issues frequently remain unaddressed. When they join voices with other groups, their issues are harder to ignore.

REFLECTION POINTS

- What resources related to healthcare have been lost in your community?
- What economic changes have affected your community and affected the ability to provide care?
- What marginalized communities or populations exist locally? What analysis has been done to understand their healthcare needs? Do the marginalized have a voice in the direction of your organization?

- Does your organization have cultural competency training for the staff? Is it effective?

- How can telemedicine be used to fill the gaps throughout your organization's service area?

- How active are you in legislative advocacy?

REFERENCES

Henning-Smith, C. E., A. M. Hernandez, R. R. Hardeman, M. R. Ramirez, and K. B. Kozhimannil. 2019. "Rural Counties with Majority Black or Indigenous Populations Suffer the Highest Rates of Premature Death in the US." *Health Affairs* 38 (12): 2019–26. https://doi.org/10.1377/hlthaff.2019.00847.

National Advisory Committee on Rural Health and Human Services. 2015. "Mortality and Life Expectancy in Rural America: Connecting the Health and Human Service Safety Nets to Improve Health Outcomes over the Life Course." Policy Brief. Published October 2015. https://www.hrsa.gov/sites/default/files/hrsa/advisory-committees/rural/2015-mortality.pdf.

CHAPTER 13

Why Rural Healthcare Leaders Get Fired

Tim Putnam, DHA, MBA, FACHE

ALL GOOD THINGS must come to an end. Being a rural healthcare leader has rewards—but also perils. There are obvious downfalls like the disapproval of one's superiors and poor financial performance, but those are common realities in healthcare leadership regardless of the setting. There are a few issues specific to rural communities—professional dangers that may not be obvious to people who "ain't from around here." It is wise to be aware of them.

CONFLICTS WITH PHYSICIANS

The medical staff is a strong force in any healthcare organization, but its force is especially vigorous in rural communities where the rural medical staff has three advantages over leadership in a dispute:

1. **Physicians are harder to recruit to the community.**
   This leaves any leader more vulnerable when a physician says to the board, "I can no longer work with this person. It's them or me." The board is put in a difficult position, knowing that open physician positions have drawn no interest and 20 applicants responded within the first week for the last CEO search.

2. **Physicians have more local longevity.** It is common for physicians to spend their entire careers in one community, whereas leaders tend to turn over much more quickly and their roots in the town don't run as deep.

3. **Physicians have strong and trusted relationships with key members of the community.** A physician can have several thousand patient interactions each year, with many of those people trusting every word they say. Even if a physician does not speak to patients directly about their displeasure with the administration, the influence they can wield is substantial, should they choose to use it.

Physicians know they possess these advantages and can instigate actions against a CEO such as a vote of no-confidence. Rarely are steps like these specifically mentioned in medical staff bylaws or other governance documents, but they are opportunities for physicians to voice their displeasure.

INTERVIEWS WITH THE PRESS

Market forces have led to the closure of many local newspapers and radio stations in rural areas, reducing healthcare leaders' access to local audiences. Meanwhile, many rural residents have begun to shun the national press for delivering "fake news." Still, healthcare leaders should be ready to respond to media inquiries, although they need to carefully think through their responses.

A willingness to discuss issues such as shrinking reimbursement rates can keep the general public and the decision-makers in government aware of what is happening in healthcare from the rural perspective. Nevertheless, it should be noted that working with the media will rarely yield benefits for the individual giving the interview. While there can be any number of outcomes for leaders when they work with the media, two can cause serious trouble.

1. **The interview goes poorly and casts the facility or team in a negative light.** The negativity may be the result of a comment taken out of context, the failure to give credit to someone who feels they deserve it, or a simple gaff. Even when 90 percent of the people who read or hear a report think it reflects positively on the hospital and the community, 10 percent with a negative reaction can harbor a grudge that is difficult to appease.

2. **The interview goes very well and is picked up regionally or nationally.** In this case, some in the community will undoubtedly accuse the leader who is interviewed of glory-seeking, which is not well-received in small towns that prefer humility. Praising the whole healthcare team in every interview can help defuse this argument.

ON THE WRONG SIDE OF THE INFLUENTIAL

Most small communities have a few influential families. Their power can come from politics, business (as employers), longevity (tracing their lineage back to the founding of the community), or sheer size. These families will wield influence over the local healthcare system that is likely both official and unofficial.

These individuals can exert an especially large span of control in small communities, as they are big fish in a small pond. The social interconnectedness in rural areas can mean one offended person can cause a leader to become a pariah very quickly. The quote from George Orwell in *Animal Farm* that "all animals are equal, but some animals are more equal than others" should be remembered by rural health leaders as they try to navigate the labyrinth of rural communities. Awareness of those who are more equal can be very useful.

The clearest danger for a rural healthcare leader comes when a person of influence or someone whom that individual cares about has a negative experience at the hospital, either as an employee or a patient. Terminating a member of a large local family, sending one to collections for failure to pay, or even making a comment that is taken out of context could have repercussions for hospital leaders as they see their influence wane and days become numbered. This result not only is hard on the individual but also reflects negatively on their organization.

The amount of deference to give to high-profile people is difficult to say. There is no universal answer. Power players in rural communities can help bring the community together, welcome newcomers, and be great allies when facing a common challenge. However, favoritism can also damage a hospital leader's reputation and the trust of their team if they are not perceived as being fair to others. The best way to strike a balance is to develop an informal sounding board of a few trusted long-time members of the community who will speak frankly and in confidence about how to navigate these challenges when a crisis arises. These supporters can be members of the board, employees, or friends who know the community well. It is important to have this sounding board in place and ready to be called on when rumors start flying.

It seems that nearly everyone in a small town has enough cousins to watch their back and let them know when they have done something to upset the natural order. Newcomers do not have this natural network, so they must build their own.

THE PRICE OF EHR SYSTEM IMPLEMENTATION

Electronic health record (EHR) systems are vital to healthcare delivery today. In years past, physicians seemed to memorize their patients' histories and medications. Paper charts attempted to document all this information and other details. However, the chart never seemed to give a complete picture or be where it was needed, and a chart was of little use if it was locked up in the physician's office when the patient was in the emergency department. With the rise of EHR systems, the value of having information beyond what the patient is able to express is clear. The promise of a complete and easily shared EHR is great, but the reality is that EHR systems do not automatically communicate smoothly with each other from office to office or hospital to hospital.

It is not uncommon for a patient to require repeat lab tests or imaging when they are transferred from a rural hospital to an urban facility. Frankly, it is a hassle for the receiving staff and it's just easier and quicker for them to repeat the test than to figure out how to access the patient's record. This is especially true when the rural facility has an antiquated EHR system that does not flow well into another EHR system or regional health information exchange (HIE).

EHR systems are one of the most unpopular topics among healthcare staff. Constant training and upgrades demand continuous efforts to understand this ever-changing tool that provides as much frustration as value for them. When EHR systems need major upgrades, several problems inevitably arise.

- The cost is substantial. The software and installation alone will cut deep into the operational and capital budget, and that is just the first check that needs to be written.
- A substantial number of staff hours must be dedicated to the development and then training on the new system.
- Clinical orders will be cumbersome for months. Regardless of how the system is built, staff will need some information quickly and be unable to find it in the new system.
- Providers may be less productive, generally reducing the number of scheduled patients for months to accommodate the extra time needed to adjust to the new system.
- Every aspect of the coding and billing process is likely to break and need to be fixed more than once. Bills to Medicare, Medicaid, and every insurance company will need to be monitored and corrected quickly. It is common to see the days in accounts receivable climb and the collections shrink for months after a new EHR implementation.

All these issues will result in a strain on the financial health and morale of the organization. Implementing or upgrading a new EHR system is never convenient and usually comes when all options to keep the old system running are exhausted.

Ultimate responsibility for the EHR system falls on the leadership team. That fact is simply unavoidable. When the financials are worse than last year, patient volume drops, and clinical staff is upset about spending more time at the computer than with the patient, memories of past hassles with the paper system will be forgotten and only the face of the leaders who made the EHR system change will come to mind. Decisions will be questioned and accusations will be made: *Another system should have been chosen. The implementation was poorly planned.* Frustrated people will look for vengeance, and the organization's leadership will be the obvious target. Given the close working relationships in rural areas, the frustration can get personal.

Rural healthcare leaders are well-advised to keep two points in mind as they face the inevitable prospect of a stressful EHR system upgrade:

1. **Communicate early and often exactly how much of a disruption the project will cause.** Leadership must make a strong case that the update is vital to the organization's continuing ability to provide care—and that all must commit to the common good. The clinical staff should be involved in the choice of the system (and, when they complain later, be reminded that they were involved). The time frame to achieve optimal operations with the new system—from 18–24 months— must be clearly stated.

2. **Expect carnage and blame to fall on leadership.** It may be wise to develop an exit strategy to execute in case it becomes necessary to leave the organization after an especially contentious implementation. Ideally, the next leader should be able to start with a clean slate. If possible,

a change in leadership should be delayed until the new system is up and running.

REFLECTION POINTS

- What can you or your board do to help leaders who face professional challenges?

- What happens in your organization when there is a disagreement between a physician and leadership that makes the relationship untenable? Who holds more authority in such a situation?

- What are the reactions in your community when your organization gets attention from local, regional, or national press? What is your tolerance for working with the media?

- When was your organization's last EHR system implementation? What lessons were learned? When is the next major technology change planned?

Case Studies

Tim Putnam, DHA, MBA, FACHE

THESE CASE STUDIES are intended to create discussion, stir debate, and identify different opinions and approaches to rural healthcare in a variety of contexts. As the hypothetical cases described here demonstrate, the rural healthcare leader's role is not for the faint of heart—the problems are all too common and cannot be escaped by just moving to another town. Sometimes, the best approach may not resolve the issue but keep it from exploding and causing collateral damage.

AN AMBULANCE SERVICE EMERGENCY

Waterville Community Hospital is an independent critical access hospital in the Great Plains. It has a reputation for quality and enjoys a solid connection to its community. By rural hospital standards, it is financially solid with 75 days of cash on hand and a low turnover of staff. However, the past two years have been difficult, with losses of 3 percent each year and a drop in cash reserves due to necessary capital investments.

The hospital has an excellent working relationship with the city's emergency medical services (EMS) provider. The hospital's emergency department (ED) staff and the city's paramedics respect each other and make a great team. The ambulance crew frequently stays after bringing in a patient to assist the ED staff with the most complex cases.

When no local paramedics are available to cover 911 calls, other ambulance services in the region can transport patients but may need more than 6 hours to respond.

On average, only one or two patients a day may require a transfer to a higher level of care. However, the number of transfers can be as high as eight in one day, with as many as three at the same time. This does not cover the possibility of mass casualty situations such as shootings or bus wrecks that would require many more rapid transfers.

Several factors have changed over the past year to complicate the situation.

1. The hospital has contracted with an emergency room (ER) physicians group to save costs. Unfortunately, this group transfers more and admits fewer patients than the previous physicians, with 10–15 additional patient transfers a month. When questioned about the trend, the ER physicians respond that many previous patients should have been transferred and that the administration should not challenge their clinical judgment. As a result, paramedics frequently struggle to explain to patients why they must be taken to a distant hospital for care. Also, the ER physicians are not friendly to the EMS staff and instead offer blunt critiques of the care they provide in the field. The EMS staff follow protocols and are frustrated by the criticism, as the ER physicians make no attempt to change the protocols or to improve the training.

2. With a large service area and low volume, EMS have been running at a sizable financial loss that is subsidized by the city. Now, the mayor informs the fire chief that the subsidy needs to be trimmed in the coming year. Additionally, the city council will not approve the planned purchase of a new ambulance. The reasoning is that the

city's current ambulances will last longer if they do not provide the transfer service. The mayor suggests that the fire chief should focus on 911 responses; transfers from the local hospital will no longer be the city's responsibility.

3. Local paramedic attrition is accelerating. The loss of staff is due in part to increases in hospital transfers—the least favorite runs for the EMS crews, who prefer the shorter 911 calls. They are reluctant to take hospital transfer calls and are becoming more vocal about it. The friction with the contract ER physicians adds fuel to this fire.

Citing the budget cuts and staffing issues, the fire chief informs the hospital leadership team that he can no longer provide hospital transfers and gives 30 days' notice. The most viable way to continue the service may be for the hospital to cover the shortfall, purchase a new ambulance, and fund an on-call premium for the EMS staff. This would amount to $225,000 for a fully equipped ambulance and an annual subsidy of around $300,000. Creating the hospital's own ambulance transfer service would be nearly double this amount and run at an annual net loss of more than $300,000. It would also mean trying to recruit EMS staff away from the city, as they are the only EMS staff in the region—creating more friction with the city.

The fire chief says the city might go for the first option if the hospital CEO and board chair approach the mayor with their proposal. The chief adds that the friction between the paramedics and the ER hospitalists is concerning and needs to be resolved as well.

Questions for Discussion

1. What is the impact on hospital staff and patients if they must wait several hours for an ambulance to arrive from outside the region?

2. How can the friction between the contract ER hospitalists and the EMS team be resolved?

3. What are the political implications for the fire chief if he tries to work with the hospital instead of simply following through with the mayor's order?

4. Hospital leadership decides to subsidize the city's EMS transfers.

   a. How should the mayor be approached? Who in the community might be most helpful in finding a solution that would be acceptable to both the hospital and the city?

   b. What current hospital services should be cut to cover the costs of subsidizing the city EMS or creating a new transfer service?

PHYSICIAN ON THE EDGE

Green Valley Regional Hospital (GVRH) is a community hospital. Sam Grant, a primary care physician at the hospital who grew up in the community, has earned decent quality scores but can be rough on the staff. He demands the best care for his patients and gets extremely upset when he believes they are at risk from poor care from the healthcare team.

His frustration comes and goes, but he seems more isolated and less cordial lately. The CNO and director of quality have made the CEO aware of a sharp increase in Dr. Grant's improper behavior. In one instance, he told a joke that made some nurses feel uncomfortable. A recent incident in the staff lounge particularly disappointed the CNO: Dr. Grant brought a staff member to tears while scolding her for not properly changing a patient's dressing. The other nurses present filed a report about the incident, calling his action "unprofessional and degrading." Staff throughout the hospital is talking about Dr. Grant as he continues to undermine morale. Also, the

CNO is aware of a "very friendly" relationship between Dr. Grant and a new member of the clinic staff. They are coordinating their schedules to have lunch together regularly.

Dr. Grant's brother, Lou, is a member of Green Valley Regional's board of trustees. He tells the CEO that his physician brother has been having issues with support staff, whose lack of competence is creating a stressful environment for all the physicians, specifically his brother. Lou says that the stress from work is affecting his brother's marriage and family life. Lou is dissatisfied when the CEO promises to look into the issues—he wants a swifter response: "Make an example of someone today and send a message, or the board will be forced to take action."

The CEO and CMO quickly meet with Dr. Grant to discuss his concerns about the staff, as well as their concerns about his outbursts. Dr. Grant becomes defensive and says he is being ganged up on for wanting only the best for his patients. He denies being hard on the staff; he says he gives constructive criticism that should be appreciated. He leaves the meeting abruptly, stating, "I'm an employee, so you can fire me if you want to, but I'm going to make sure everyone knows that neither of you cares about improving quality."

Questions for Discussion

1. What conflicts of interest exist? How can they be resolved?
2. What resources does the CEO have to resolve or temper the situation?
3. When should the board get involved in personnel decisions?
4. How should Dr. Grant's behavior with the staff be investigated and addressed?
5. How much of the background should the CEO share with the board? What is likely to be Lou's response?

A BROKEN RELATIONSHIP

Chuck Smith, a board member of Small Town Hospital, is a successful business owner and well-regarded by the community. One day, he is in the park playing with his grandson, and the child falls from the monkey bars. Chuck takes him to the ER, and he is told the injury is a sprain. The next day, a radiologist views the image, sees a clear break, and notifies the family. The parents take him to Big City Hospital, where the orthopedic surgeon is outraged by the misdiagnosis and states the boy will need surgery. Moreover, because of the delay, there could be further damage—only time will tell. He tells the parents that he is not familiar with Small Town Hospital, but they should avoid it.

Chuck has been a strong public advocate for Small Town Hospital, but he is now convinced that he put his grandson at risk by taking him there. He openly voices concerns about the hospital, based on his grandson's experience. The board chair and CEO assure Chuck that the situation is being taken seriously and encourage him to tone down his public statements. The chief of staff tells Chuck that what happened to his grandson could also have happened at Big City Hospital. Chuck is unmoved. After requesting a meeting with the CEO at Big City Hospital, Chuck learns that they are willing to put in a free-standing ER in Small Town to provide quality care to the community. With Chuck's support, Big City Hospital will do this alone if Small Town Hospital is not willing to partner with them.

Chuck later reminds the chair that the board is responsible for Small Town Hospital's mission to improve healthcare in the community, and the hospital has failed in that responsibility. He invites Big City Hospital representatives and the public to the next Small Town Hospital board meeting, which is allowed by the state's open meetings act.

A directly competing ER in the community will significantly reduce Small Town Hospital's revenue and affect the organization's ability to survive in the long term.

Questions for Discussion

1. Should the Small Town Hospital board chair allow Big City Hospital to be on the meeting agenda? What is likely to happen if it is allowed? Or not allowed?

2. Is there any issue with Chuck meeting with the CEO at Big City Hospital?

3. Would a freestanding ER in a small community make sense? What does Big City Hospital really want?

4. What actions can be taken to appease Chuck?

5. Should Small Town Hospital's CEO contact Big City Hospital's CEO? What should be the goal of the conversation?

6. Assuming that the situation with Chuck's grandson is being taken seriously and is under quality review, what other action should the CEO take?

MAKING CHANGES IN PAYER CONTRACTING

Washington Community Hospital (WCH) is struggling to remain financially viable. It has experienced losses averaging 2 percent over the past three years and has only 20 days of cash reserves with a limited ability to borrow funds to continue operations. Even after budget cuts and improvement projects, the board and leadership are very concerned about the future if the financial situation does not improve soon.

The strong and united clinical staff members are proud of the care they provide for their friends and neighbors. They take the community's needs seriously with programs to combat addiction, depression, and diabetes—all reflecting best practices for community hospitals in the state.

Total Blew Insurance (TBI), WCH's largest commercial insurance payer, informs the hospital that it wants to move it to the standard payment plan based on Medicare charges. For WCH, this move will result in a 10 percent decrease in revenue.

Southern Pine Construction (SPC) is the largest employer in the area and a TBI client. The company's CFO contacts the hospital to express concerns about healthcare costs. The company's insurance rates have gone up each of the previous four years and are becoming unaffordable. The insurer blames the high rates on the hospital's charges and offers SPC a 5 percent discount to go into the preferred provider network with the healthcare system 40 miles away in a larger community. The CFO does not want to switch, as most employees are local and prefer to use WCH. But the fiscal reality is that the company cannot continue to pay such high rates and may need to change to TBI's preferred provider network. The CFO encourages the hospital to work with the insurer to ensure local coverage for SPC employees.

Later at the local chamber of commerce meeting, a representative from the state chamber shares an update on businesses' struggles with health insurance costs. She presents a report that shows the state pays more for health insurance than other states because of hospitals' high prices. Washington Community Hospital's CEO and CFO are at the meeting and find it odd that the state chamber is accusing not-for-profit hospitals of creating the problem while insurance companies report record profits. Due to time constraints, they are not allowed to present an immediate rebuttal.

Back at the office, the hospital's leadership team considers TBI's proposal and makes three determinations.

1. Under the proposed terms, the hospital should see an increase in volume in some outpatient areas because TBI has been encouraging patients to go to the preferred provider network for some tests. Supposedly, this practice would stop under the new agreement.

2. TBI would be able to offer a lower insurance cost to customers and achieve a strategic advantage over other

insurers. However, as TBI captures more of the market, other insurance companies will demand a similar reduction in rates, thus creating a race-to-the-bottom pricing scenario.

3. It's difficult to project how many of SPC's employees would go elsewhere for care if the company joined the insurer's preferred network. WCH would likely lose some volume but retain much of it. A negative impact on the hospital's finances is indicated, although the degree of significance is difficult to determine.

Questions for Discussion

1. What strategy should the hospital employ in negotiating insurance rates? Should it accept the TBI proposal?
2. How could the hospital engage local employers in its effort to negotiate with TBI?
3. Diabetes, addiction, and depression programs save lives but operate at a net loss. Must WCH cut these programs to remain financially viable, or are there alternatives? What are the implications of these programs being discontinued?
4. What are some local implications of employees leaving town for care?
5. What other resources could be accessed to improve the hospital's financial condition?

THE NEW SHERIFF IN TOWN

Deer Valley Health Center (DVHC) is a federally qualified health center (FQHC) that operates three clinics. The total service area population is 8,000 with no major employer. Most DVHC patients are covered by Medicare or Medicaid, but the FQHC designation has enabled it to remain financially viable. Community leaders formed DVHC 10 years ago when the last physician in the region retired.

Patients who need a higher level of care are sent to one of two regional community hospitals. River Hill Hospital (RHH) and Timber Meadow Hospital (TMH)—are both 40 minutes away in opposite directions. DVHC has enjoyed good working relationships with the hospitals and has sent patients to them for care when necessary

Things have changed with the recent arrival of Joe Gardner. In his first three months as CEO at TMH, he brought on an entirely new leadership team and made other changes that affect DVHC.

- He canceled a diabetes partnership dedicated to education, nutrition, funding for prescriptions, and remote monitoring.
- He opted out of a joint grant application for EMS paramedicine that would fund home visits.
- He launched an aggressive social media and marketing campaign in Deer Valley to encourage patients to come to TMH for "superior" primary care.

Concerned about these moves, the board of directors at DVHC encouraged their CEO, Tina Palmer, to repair the relationship. As one board member noted, they could not afford to lose such an important partner.

In her meeting at Timber Meadow, Tina learns a lot about Joe's way of doing business.

- He sees himself as a strictly business-minded leader who runs a fiscally responsible operation. He is unapologetic about canceling programs and partnerships, citing his fiduciary responsibility to TMH.
- He is proud of his new leadership team's business acumen. He is pleased that people know there is a new sheriff

in town who has quickly "hired some, fired some, and painted the lobby."

- He points to the construction of a state-of-the-art hyperbaric wound program to treat diabetic patients as a sign of TMH's new focus on treatments and procedures, specifically those with a high return on investment. He believes that where there is no margin, there is no mission—and margin must come first.

- He is disappointed that DVHC does not refer more patients to TMH and that those who are referred are not well-insured, dismissing the fact that the referrals reflect the overall payer mix in Deer Valley.

- He is certain that Tina is recruiting members of his staff and considers any such poaching to be an aggressive act. (In fact, DVMC is not recruiting TMH staff but has seen several applications. Now that she has met Joe, she knows why they want to leave.)

- He makes it clear that if DVHC ever sees the need to become part of a high-quality regional health system, his door at TMH is open for that discussion.

Tina is flabbergasted by Joe's perspective. The other healthcare leaders in the region agree with her that there is no pot of gold for healthcare providers in their rural communities. Their conversations always revolve around ways to work together to improve the health of the people they serve. Joe seems to see patients as customers who should improve the hospital's bottom line, which is difficult for her to comprehend. She thinks of patients as her friends and neighbors, not as sources of revenue.

Tina later reaches out to Kelly Roth, CEO at RHH, the other community hospital in the region. Tina shares that TMH has discontinued some important joint programs. While Kelly assures Tina that his hospital's working relationship with DVHC remains strong, RHH is dealing with its own financial pressures and cannot pick up the programs that TMH discontinued at this time.

Questions for Discussion

1. Has Joe Gardner crossed any legal lines in his dealings with DVHC? If so, how should Tina respond?

2. What information from the meeting with Joe should Tina share with her board?

3. How seriously should Tina take Joe's offer to discuss DVMC joining TMH?

4. Should Tina do anything to address Joe's comment about the local payer mix?

5. Tina is disappointed with Joe's approach to healthcare. How open should she be about her opinion with the board? With her leadership team? What are the likely outcomes if she shares her opinion?

6. How should DVHC react to TMH's decision to opt out of their diabetes and EMS partnerships?

7. Should DVHC consider hiring nurses and physicians at TMH who have applied for open positions? What are the implications of hiring them? What are the implications of making a practice of not hiring them?

8. Is there a middle ground where Tina and Joe can work together? Should Tina try to find a middle ground?

Index

About the Authors

Tim Putnam, DHA, MBA, FACHE, has worked in healthcare since 1983, initially in laser/minimally invasive surgery research and later as CEO at hospitals in Illinois and Indiana. Most recently, he served as CEO of Margaret Mary Health in Batesville, Indiana, one of the largest critical access hospitals in the United States. He received his doctorate in health administration from the Medical University of South Carolina, where his dissertation was on acute stroke care in rural hospitals. He is a past president of the National Rural Health Association and Indiana Rural Health Association. A lifelong learner, Dr. Putnam was certified as an emergency medical technician in 2015 and worked for his community's emergency medical service (EMS). Dr. Putnam lectures nationally on rural healthcare improvement, the transition from volume to value, rural graduate medical education, EMS, and health equity. President Biden appointed him in 2021 to the COVID-19 Health Equity Task Force, for which he chaired the Healthcare Access and Quality subcommittee.

Nikki King, DHA, was born and raised in the coal fields of southeastern Kentucky. She is the CEO of Alliance Health in Fort Wayne, Indiana. Before working in healthcare, she worked for the Center for Business and Economic Research, where she studied models of sustainability in rural communities with a single economic engine. Dr. King has worked in the population health, clinical statistics, and health administration fields, developing high-quality, low-cost models of care for high-acuity individuals. She serves on the Indiana

Rural Health Association's board of directors, the National Rural Health Association's Policy Congress and Government Affairs Committee, and chairs the Rural Health Leadership Radio board of directors. Dr. King obtained her bachelor's degree in economics from the University of Kentucky, master's degree in health services administration from Xavier University, and doctorate in healthcare administration from the Medical University of South Carolina.

Bill Auxier, PhD, grew up in the rural Midwest. For his introduction to healthcare, he worked at the local hospital as a nurse's aide while in high school. He went on to a career in medical devices and services and was eventually named CEO of a global surgical device manufacturer. He holds a bachelor's degree in business, a master's degree in communication, and a doctorate in leadership. Dr. Auxier combined his real-world experience and academic training to establish the Auxier Group and Center for Rural Health Leadership.

Contributor

Benjamin Anderson is vice president for rural health and hospitals at the Colorado Hospital Association. Previously, he served as CEO of Kearny County Hospital in Lakin, Kansas. Anderson is a recognized leader in transforming rural healthcare through a mission-driven approach to recruiting physicians to underserved areas. He has been named to *Becker's Hospital Review's* list of Rising Stars of healthcare leaders under 40 and *Modern Healthcare's* list of Up & Comers. He earned a bachelor's degree in English and a master's degree in business administration from Drury University and a master's degree in healthcare delivery science from Dartmouth College.